SEAWEED, SALMON, *and* MANZANITA CIDER

A California Indian Feast

A Southern California Indian feast, early 1900s. Photo courtesy of the Braun Research Library, Autry National Center, #P2096.

SEAWEED, SALMON, and MANZANITA CIDER

▼

A California Indian Feast

Edited by Margaret Dubin and Sara-Larus Tolley

Heyday Books, Berkeley, California

Library of Congress Cataloging-in-Publication Data
Seaweed, salmon, and Manzanita cider : a California Indian feast / edited
by Margaret Dubin and Sara-Larus Tolley.
    p. cm.
  ISBN 978-1-59714-078-2 (pbk. : alk. paper)
  1. Indian cookery. 2. Indians of North America--Food--California. 3.
Indians of North America--California--Social life and customs. I. Dubin,
Margaret Denise. II. Tolley, Sara-Larus, 1973-
  TX715.S145725 2008
  641.59'2970794--dc22
                        2008003025

Book Design: Rebecca LeGates
Printed in China by Everbest Printing Co. through Four Colour Imports,
Ltd., Louisville, Kentucky

Orders, inquiries, and correspondence should be addressed to:
    Heyday Books
    P. O. Box 9145, Berkeley, CA 94709
    (510) 549-3564, Fax (510) 549-1889
    www.heydaybooks.com

10 9 8 7 6 5 4 3 2 1

CONTENTS

MEAT

VEGETABLES

BERRIES, FRUITS, and FLOWERS

NUTS and SEEDS

ACORNS

ACKNOWLEDGMENTS

Salmon smoked and kippered by the late "Snooks" Marshall (Hupa) and canned by Erma Marshall (Karuk). Photo by Scott Braley.

This book is the product of many years of friendships and cultural sharing. Margaret would like to thank Beverly R. Ortiz for her commitment to accurate and sensitive representation of the people; Renee Shahrokh for her sage editing advice and for sharing her interview transcripts; Ira Jacknis for generously sharing the manuscript of his book *Food in California Indian Culture* before it was publicly available; Dale Noel and Geno Lucich for teaching her husband how to spear-fish salmon (he didn't catch any); and Bradley Marshall for his unflagging support, good humor, and superlative canned salmon (his mother's, actually), which made up for our bad fishing luck. Sara would like to thank Barbara Drake for her enthusiasm, creativity, and willingness to share what goes on in her kitchen, and Ardy Reed for going above and beyond by not only telling us about her acorn mush stirrers but also making and sending one for us to keep.

Margaret Dubin and Sara-Larus Tolley

FOREWORD

KATHLEEN ROSE SMITH, YOLETAMAL/BODEGA MIWOK AND MIHILAKAWNA/DRY CREEK POMO

Before Euro-American domination, more than one thousand independent nations (including bands and tribes) thrived in the place now known as California. This place provided generously for all of them, the people whose creation narratives each winter call to mind that we were created for this land. And this land was created for us and all our relatives, everything that's natural, grand, awesome, humbling, and good—other animals, plants, rocks, waterways, and celestial beings.

To live in spiritual and physical balance in the same small area for thousands of years without feeling the need to go somewhere else, as was the case with my people, requires restraint, respect, and knowledge of the ways of each animal and plant. As my mother taught me—and she, in turn, had been taught—the plants, animals, and birds are our relatives, and we had better know how to act around them, or they'll get after us.

And so, in fact, there's abundance, but with this abundance come rules for living and behaving properly, for caretaking the land. We must not be self-centered. The world doesn't begin and end with us. We must know when to gather. We must not over-gather. We must know how to prepare foods—when to bake and when to leach, so that foods such as acorn and buckeye (my relatives called it "ice cream") become "sweet." We must approach our foods with prayer, seek permission from the plants, animals, and fish, and be grateful for their life-sustaining gift. We must contribute by giving something back for what we take. By managing the land—burning it, pruning it, and digging it properly—we enhance the growth of the plants that sustain us, and the animals upon which we rely.

California is astounding in its natural beauty. There are coastal plateaus and island enclaves; two great deserts; forested, glacial, and volcanic mountains; coastal and transverse ranges; and valleys small and vast, with many rivers, creating a delta flowing into an enormous bay rich in food for people and other animals. Our people lived in all these places, blessed with many foods, some nearby, others requiring trade to obtain. We knew (and still know) the land with an intimacy that results from countless interactions.

Our foods were (and still are) as varied as the landscape, as are our methods of preparing them. We ate them raw. We roasted, boiled, baked, leached, dried, and stored them, and, after contact, we fried, steeped, and canned them.

Mrs. Partillo, Salvadora Valenzuela, Manuel Chupensa, and Dominga Chupensa, all Cupeño, gathering for coffee, Pala, 1949. Photo by Walter Goldschmidt.

Tribes of California

Tolowa
Yurok
Chilula
Whilkut
Wiyot
Bear River
Mattole
Lassik
Sinkyone
Cahto
Coast Miwok
Esselen

Karuk
Shasta
Hupa
Tsnungwe
Chimariko
Nongatl
Wintu
Wailaki
Nomlaki
Yuki
Konkow
Patwin
Lake Miwok
Wappo
Plains Miwok
Pomo

Modoc
Pit River Tribes (includes Itam'is, Aw'te, Atsugewi)
Northern Paiute (Paviotso)
Yana
Maidu
Washoe
Nisenan
Sierra Mewuk
Mono Paiute
Yokuts
Owens Valley Paiute
Ohlone
Chukchansi
Mono
Panamint Shoshone
Salinan
Tubatulabal
Kawaiisu
Chemehuevi
Yowlumni
Kitanemuk
Chumash
Serrano
Mojave
Fernandeño/Tataviam
Tongva (Gabrielino)
Ajachmem (Juaneño)
Cahuilla
Halchidhoma
Cupeño
Luiseño (Payoomkawichum)
Ipai
Kumeyaay
Quechan (Yuma)

Today acorn is our most well-known food. However, before the Euro-American invasion, the roasted, ground seeds of dozens of plants, including bunchgrasses, were the food of choice for many of our nations. Called *yuhu* in my Dry Creek Pomo language, also known as *pinole*, some of these seeds are now hard to come by. Many of the plants that produce them no longer exist, are rare, or can't be accessed, so now we must substitute purchased, raw grains, mostly wheat. Although still sweet, wheat lacks the nutty taste of the older grains and seeds.

Our foods are varied, delicious, and served in some of the finest eateries in the world—foods such as abalone, mussels, oysters, clams, sea urchins, sea anemones, turban snails, duck, goose, quail, venison, elk, rabbit, salmon, trout, seaweed, hazelnuts, black walnuts, watercress, and native berries, including strawberries, raspberries, blackberries, and huckleberries. Less renowned but utterly tasty Native California foods include mud hen, robins, various small game, China shoe (like abalone without the shell), sturgeon, surf fish, the roe of all the various caught fish, thimbleberries, manzanita berry *yuhu*, peppernuts, buckeye, elephant ears (tree mushrooms), bulbs, grass nuts, native onions, celery (angelica tops), yerba buena tea, and tree tea (coast tea).

Some of our indigenous foods are now threatened by modern development and diseases. In some cases, access to traditional gathering grounds is denied by public or private landowners; in the case of acorn, a disease called sudden oak death, which affects many species, is killing some of our most important acorn-producing plants, the tan oak and black oak.

Supplementing the old-time cuisine are introduced and so-called survival foods, including black mustard greens,

tortillas, *tuptup* (a puffy bread made of wheat flour and water, baked in an oven or cooked on coals or embers), *pucklone* (boiled wheat dough), beans, rice, lard, fried potatoes, fry bread, flank (Indian meat), slab bacon, coffee, homemade fruit and vegetable preserves, *zahtza* (spiced green tomato preserve), and, more recently, federal surplus foods, such as dried and evaporated milk, powdered eggs, pasteurized cheese, and canned meats and beans. These so-called commodity foods leave much to be desired nutritionally, but have nonetheless been integrated into many Native California diets.

Despite missionization, Mexican land grants, the Russian quest for sea otters, and American expansionism, we are still here. And despite urbanization, privatization, agribusiness, water removal, and pollution, our foods are still here as well. This book celebrates our endurance by providing you with a savory glimpse of the many traditional foods we continue to enjoy.

Kathleen Rose Smith gathering seaweed, 1991. Photo by Beverly R. Ortiz.

Elizabeth Enos (Nisenan Maidu) peeling and mashing buckeyes, 1960. Photos by Samuel A. Barrett, courtesy of the Phoebe Apperson Hearst Museum of Anthropology and the Regents of the University of California, #25-5034 and 25-5042.

INTRODUCTION

MARGARET DUBIN AND SARA-LARUS TOLLEY

This is a cookbook, but not in any conventional sense. Traditional cultures did not write down, or even necessarily commit to memory, instructions for food preparation, which meant that even simple meals tasted different when prepared at different times by different cooks. Like stories that change slightly each time they are told, meals like acorn mush or fish stew vary in taste and texture depending on what ingredients are available, how they are harvested or gathered, and who prepares them.

In our effort to document and share the vibrant culture of California Indian foods, we contacted Native people throughout the state and asked them to contribute recipes, essays, and photographs to this book. Everyone was enthusiastic about the project, but some found it difficult to "put down" their family's recipes; as Linda Santiago Peterson (Yokuts/Yowlumni) explained, "We used a pinch of this, a handful of that, whatever was in season with a few store-bought staples." She went on to describe her mother and aunts telling how, in their younger days, they would get squirrels from the cats and "poke a little hole in them to get the guts out and then throw them in the fire to singe the hair and hide off." She reminisced a little while longer about baked rattlesnake, fried tree mushrooms, deer meat, and a dish her mother made with fried bacon bits, potatoes, onions, and fresh watercress. Then she had to stop talking because she was getting too hungry. And so the "recipes" in this book should not be considered exact directions for a traditional cuisine; rather, they are transcriptions from tribal and personal memory and, as such, fragments of living culture.

We have not attempted to represent the whole of traditional California Indian cuisine, but rather to present a selection of some of the foods and preparations we thought readers might find interesting or useful. Foods that have been omitted include insects, which were eaten raw or roasted, or used to make salad dressing; salt, of which two forms were known, rock salt and salt derived from marsh grasses; and many small birds and game animals.

Because they are easily available elsewhere, we decided not to include recipes for the now-ubiquitous fry bread and tortilla. These are prime examples of what Kathleen Rose Smith calls introduced foods—in the early days, government-issued foods and foods served at boarding schools, and later all kinds of commercially available foods. These

foods overwhelmed the California Indian diet and, in many cases, contributed to new and serious health problems (what Luiseño/Cupeño writer Gordon Johnson calls "commod bod"), such as obesity and diabetes. Some introduced foods, such as wheat flour, beans, and chili peppers, have found important places in tribal diets, as have cultivated fruits and vegetables, without eliminating traditional foods. In fact, in many places traditional foods are prized even more than in the recent past, used symbolically or ceremonially on special occasions.

Traditional foods are especially precious today because different kinds of intrusions have limited tribal peoples' access to them. The diversion of water for agriculture has resulted in massive salmon kills in the northern part of the state, in which thousands of fish sicken and die before they are able to reach their spawning grounds. Sudden oak death disease has decreased the state's acorn harvest, and pesticides make it dangerous to gather plant materials in many places. State fish and game laws regulate what kinds of animals can be "taken," and when and how; this can result in charges of poaching and other misdemeanors for hunters and fishermen who don't follow the rules. In 2000, Dale Noel and John "Geno" Lucich, both Maidu, were arrested by a fish and game warden for using handmade wooden spears to catch salmon in the Feather River south of Oroville. State law prohibits the use of nets, traps, or spears on the river, and neither man had obtained a special permit. The following year Lucich obtained special permits for more than fifteen tribal fishermen, and once again set up camp at the river and used his handmade spears to catch salmon (it is much harder than it looks).

Left: Salt deposit, Salt Point. Photo by Laurel Peña.

Dale Noel, left, and Danny DeLeon, both Maidu, display the salmon they caught with handmade spears on September 22, 2001. DeLeon was one of several tribal members to receive a special permit from the California Department of Fish and Game to spearfish for salmon that weekend. Photo by Margaret Dubin.

Using traditional tools to fish or hunt is only one aspect of a growing movement to relearn traditional food ways. The goal is not to return to a historic lifestyle, but to integrate traditional, healthier foods and the processes and attitudes associated with these foods into a modern lifestyle. As Hillary Renick (Fort Bragg Pomo/Paviotso Paiute) wrote in one of her many letters to us, foods like acorn and seaweed keep tribal people healthy in more ways than one: "The dramatic change in diet and the internalized racism have made Native American people sick…There is a lot of healing that Native people have to do, and I think that learning about Native foods and having pride in oneself are important parts of this."

Traditional foods are present at most contemporary California Indian gatherings. At the annual California Indian Basketweavers Association gatherings, acorn soup-cooking demonstrations draw large crowds of onlookers, Native and non-Native alike, who marvel as the acorn flour-and-water mixture boils and congeals into porridge in an old handwoven cooking basket heated only with hot rocks. "We are hungry for traditional foods, the foods of our people," elaborated Monique Sonoquie (Chumash) as she sampled freshly made acorn porridge from a small Dixie cup, "just like many of us are hungry for our cultures, songs, dances, and ceremonies." For Monique, praying and eating go hand in hand, and eating traditional foods, especially foods one has had to work hard or travel far to obtain, satisfies a hunger for life. Traditional foods also accompany Native Californians on journeys outside the state—as shown in this photograph of a salmon cookout at a political protest in Omaha, Nebraska—becoming symbolic of cultures at large and tribal sovereignty.

These are timeless foods: they can be prepared traditionally, or they can be prepared in a more modern way, on the stove. They can be covered in cream, fifties-style, or they can go nineties—"California cuisine." And like the pages of the magazine—*News from Native California*—from which it sprung, this book is a virtual gathering of the California Indian community, a snapshot in time of the people, places, and activities that make this community one of the strongest and most vibrant in the country. Yes, this is a book about food, but it is also much more: it is a book about people, people whose traditional foods shaped the lives of their ancestors and continue to bring joy, pride, and good flavor to their lives in the present.

Julia Parker (Coast Miwok/Kashaya Pomo) kneads tortilla dough, then cooks tortillas on an outdoor grill, 1991. Photos by Beverly R. Ortiz.

Above: Bryan Colegrove (Hupa) tends a salmon cookout under an interstate overpass in Omaha, Nebraska, where Karuk, Yurok, and Hupa activists joined commercial fishermen and environmentalists at the annual shareholders' meeting of Berkshire Hathaway in May 2007. The company, whose headquarters are in Omaha, controls dams on the Klamath River. Photo by Regina Chichizola.

Right: Julie Tex (Dunlap Band of Mono Indians) cooks acorn porridge with hot rocks at the California Indian Basketweavers Association annual gathering, June 23, 2006. Photo by Dugan Aguilar.

Manzanita berries. Photo by Deborah Small.

SEAWEED, SALMON, *and* MANZANITA CIDER

A California Indian Feast

FISH

Fish—especially salmon—has been a prized food and important staple for many California Indian tribes for thousands of years. Before the arrival of missionaries and American colonizers, streams and rivers teemed with salmon from Big Sur to the Oregon border, and tribal people flourished with and celebrated the bounty. Through trade, salmon also reached inland and southern tribes.

Like other fish and, indeed, many other kinds of food, salmon were harvested with great care and respect. Villages along the Klamath River, for instance, built temporary fish dams that were steeped in ritual. They were torn down exactly ten days after their construction was completed, effectively allowing the fish to move upstream to other tribes and to spawn. Today, some people use dip nets, others gill nets to catch salmon. Some tribes have hatcheries that share the fish with tribal members as well as distant cousins and friends, the fish traveling around the state in coolers and in the back of pickup trucks.

Salmon are born in the rivers and instinctively drawn to the ocean. Later, they are called back up from the sea to breed and, finally, die in the very places they were born. Interestingly, the opposite is true of eels: they are born in the ocean and make their way upstream. Sonny Ferris (Karuk/Yurok) comments, "I love to hook them in the surf. It's fun running around there when the breakers are coming in. You get wet and rolled around sometimes."

The ancient, whiskered sturgeon once navigated the California river bottoms in greater numbers than today—this single species provided not only an enormous amount of food, but a glue that could be made from the cartilage in its head. Today, the Karuk and Yurok tribes often eat sturgeon rolled in flour and seasoned with salt and pepper, preferably straight from a cast-iron frying pan.

Sucker fish were caught by the Wintu on the McCloud and Sacramento Rivers. The fish were lured into nets with weighted tree boughs angled into the water from the banks. Indeed, fishing is associated with much beautiful and intricate material culture: harpoons, hooks of bone and shell, and nets of myriad fibers.

Dams and other large-scale water resource projects have led to the loss of much of the state's wild fish population, but California Indian people still fish for livelihood, pleasure, and sustenance; fishing is a practice knotted tightly to their cultures. Trapping, netting, or hooking eel and fish is more than just "work"—it involves great parties of families camping near beach fires, eating together, and enjoying the water.

Salmon roasting at the Yurok Salmon Festival in Klamath on August 20, 2006. Photo by Ira Nowinski.

Ye'Ja

DARRYL BABE WILSON (SUL'MA'EJOTE), ITAMI'IS/AW'TE

SPLASH!

In the morning darkness the river rippled and swirled with *allis*. Often they catapulted out of the water, splashing back with a "smack!" They gathered. They labored. They loved. They spawned.

The clean sound shook the silence within the roundhouse. Alert, the young singers moved throughout the village waking the people. Warriors grabbed their spears and nets. Children screamed with joy. Warrior singers celebrated. Sparks flew within the roundhouse as the women dropped wood upon the slumbering embers. Then every portion of life in the world was focused upon the ancient churning, the *allis* river ballet, as if a giant unseen hand stirred the river with love.

Wadakjosi to the east was a silhouette. Morning Star was just struggling over the horizon. *Chool* raced in the early darkness, running away, it is said, from the sun. North Star forever weaved the glittering basket and the sparkling mystery. Darkness was all around. But the excitement of the returning salmon and the dancing fires was such a completeness that the tribal people rushed in a soft panic. The families of the young singers cried quietly with pride, others dreamed a deeper dream.

Always the people stood amazed upon the banks of the river. They saw the ripples, the swirl of the mighty river caused by the power of *allis*. There were flips and splashes. There were splashes echoing from downriver. Otter swam nearby. From the treetops eagles feathered the wind, smelling the life and sensing the freshness in the river.

Men rushed to gather *allis*. Women rushed to prepare camp. Others rushed to gather materials to begin the delicate session of smoking and preserving *allis*. Children raced with their dogs barking. Soon there would be no hunger. Fresh roe would be cooked on a flat, hot rock. Dripping, fat slices of *allis* would cook against a friendly fire. The people were ready to feast. And the people and *allis* obeyed the instructions of an earth made good in its original design.

My great-grandmother hugged her mother and father in her small arms. The little family whispered a prayer to the power that turns the earth around the sun and the sun around that wonder that is greater than wisdom and knowledge.

Old Man Coyote yodeled from a distant range. The wolf pack, yellow eyes flashing, studied the world and were thankful for *ye'ja*. Deer twitched their tails and melted into the forest. Bear tossed their huge heads, smelled the life in the river, and ambled with confidence to their favorite fishing place. Mountain Lion slipped through the trees like a whisper of yesterday.

The whole world was alive and it seemed that there would be goodness forever.

Editors' note: Ye'ja translates roughly as "personal song," a song used by common people to help a doctor in his healing ceremony.

Dugout redwood canoes made by Glen Moore (Yurok). Photo by Laurel Peña.

for three days before and
after summer's new and full moons
beneath ripples near the head of the
    Russian
bass will spawn beside sandbars
—*William Oandasan, Yuki*

Right: "Old Ned" (Karuk) repairing a net. Photo courtesy of the Huntington Library, San Marino, California.

Opposite page: A lush riparian canopy shades the deep pools where salmon await more rain before migrating upstream into the headwaters to spawn. Lagunitas Creek, West Marin County, April 2008. Photo by Paola Bouley.

Salmon Cooked on a Redwood Stick

BRADLEY MARSHALL, HUPA

Cut cleaned salmon into long chunks. Run pointed sticks through them, lengthwise, just below the skin. Build a manzanita fire and arrange sticks in the ground around the fire. As the salmon cooks it develops a crust. Check it to make sure it doesn't cook too long and fall into the fire.

Above: Gary Markusson's (Yurok/Karuk) smokehouse. Photo by Margaret Dubin. Opposite page: Merk Oliver (Yurok) tending the salmon roast at the Yurok Salmon Festival in Klamath on August 20, 2006. Photo by Ira Nowinski.

Kippered Salmon and Smoked Salmon

BRADLEY MARSHALL, HUPA

Cut cleaned salmon into long, half-inch-thick strips. Add salt and pepper to taste. Loop a string around each strip and hang from the rafters of the smokehouse. The smokehouse should be ready, with just light smoke coming from the embers of the fire. Use a fruitwood, like apple or pear, or manzanita for the fire. Keep the fire down to smoke; if there are flames the fish will cook too fast and come off the skin. Smoke the fish two to three days (depending on the heat of the fire), until it is cooked outside but still raw inside. Remove the strips from the smokehouse, cut into pieces, and put into sterilized canning jars right away. Seal the jars in a pressure cooker, where the salmon will finish cooking. You can add red chili pepper or other condiments before sealing.

For smoked salmon, cut and hang salmon as above but smoke for three or four days, depending on the heat of the fire. Remove the strips from the smokehouse and eat or store.

Medicine for Salmon

RICHARD KEELING

Editors' note: These formulas are spoken prayers that invoke the power of the woʹgey, the spirit beings who were present at the beginning of time. If brief, formulas can be recited verbatim, but they are often free-form channelings of the woʹgey, spoken or sung. In practice, formulas appear as empowered speeches or medicine-making in which a speaker petitions the woʹgey and then takes on the voice of the spirit-person to answer and activate the speaker's own prayer. The formulas described below by ethnomusicologist Richard Keeling were used as medicine by Yurok fishermen to catch salmon in the proper way. They take the form of narratives about the pre-human spirit world of the woʹgey.

Except for those used in World Renewal rituals, only four spoken formulas for taking salmon have been documented, and (probably by coincidence) all four were collected from Yurok speakers shortly after 1900.

A formula from Stone of Weitchpec (Yurok) called upon a *woʹgey* who had spoken with Nepewo, the Great Head Salmon. [The *woʹgey*] asked [Nepewo] for salmon and other things. Although he held a spear, he did not attempt to strike Nepewo, who listened and then went on his way. After that, the spirit-person always found salmon and killed them easily. The *woʹgey* who is called upon in this formula instructs the fisherman to "talk to his harpoon" (that is, speak the formula over it) and dictates various restrictions that the fisherman has to observe in order to preserve his luck.

The second formula for salmon, collected from Billy Werk of Weitchpec, was used with a song. The narrative involved a story about Small Salmon (Tserhkr). He followed some other fish into a sweathouse, even though the owner told him that there was no room to lie down there. He found himself a place anyway and sang a certain song. This formula and song were to be used while the fisherman tied the webbing to the frame of his dip net rather than after he had started fishing.

Another Yurok, known as Lame Billy of Weitchpec, had a formula for salmon involving Coyote, who pretended to be a Karuk person traveling upriver. He disguised himself as an old man and persuaded some people to take him upstream in a boat. However, he got caught while passing by the fish dam at Kepel, because someone there accused him of being the one who had run off with his wife.

The last of these formulas was explained by Barney of Sregon (Yurok). This text calls upon Pigeon, who learned how to make a net by spying on White Duck. He copied how the net was attached to the frame and learned the names for various parts of the net. Later, he got caught watching and was beaten up. That is why his chest is so narrow now; they pushed him against the ground and injured him.

Karuk fisherman. Photo courtesy of The Field Museum, #CSA9556. Inset: Merk Oliver (Yurok) tending a gill net, 1988. Photo by Jean Perry.

Traditional Pomo Fishing

JEFF JOAQUIN, HOPLAND POMO

Editors' note: With salmon and steelhead splashing up the coastal rivers every winter to spawn, and with trout, pike, suckers, hitch, and other fish crowding the waters of Clear Lake and its tributary streams, the Pomo of central California have long been blessed with plentiful freshwater fish. And they have been especially skilled at catching them—with fish dams and weirs, several different kinds of basketry traps, fish poisons such as soaproot and buckeyes, seine nets, dip nets, harpoons, and hooks and lines. In 1935, Jeff Joaquin of Hopland described some of the old ways of fishing to anthropologist F. J. Essene. Joaquin was eighty-nine at the time.

Mabel McKay (Pomo) cleaning hitch, Lake County, 1982.
Photo by Scott M. Patterson.

I remember helping to build a fish dam. A basket about four or five feet long is used. It is a funnel-shaped basket about two feet across at the large end and tapering to about four inches at the small end. The fish go into these traps of their own accord, instead of being herded in. After we completed the fish trap, all we had to do was to build a fire and watch our basket. We most generally stayed with it until we caught at least twenty fish. Then we packed them home, where they were divided among family and relations.

Before we placed these baskets in the water they were doctored by hitting them with pepperwood limbs and singing a song used for this particular occasion called "Sha-Meo-Ha-Co."

This fish trap I have been talking about was for salmon. Later in my childhood experience, when the waters were getting low in the late spring, we would use the same dam, only the basket was similar to that used for quail, but a bit smaller. This was done for catching trout. This basket was doctored or charmed the same as the basket for salmon. We did not watch the trap continually, just called for our catch once a day. The name of this basket is "La-Wame-Bio-Ha-Co."

Later, I was taught another way of catching fish. This was by digging "Sha-Chlu" (also fish poison or soap root), placing them in a sack and pounding them. Then dip the sack in the water and shake it around. The water has to be very low and still. This solution in the water makes the fish come to the top of the water. It also makes them sick or slow in action. Sometimes it killed some of the fish. This process usually made all kinds of fish fight, including salmon...

Another occupation among the men of our tribe is that of the fish diver, and here perhaps I may pause to boast that I happened to be one of these divers. These men dive underwater and catch fish of various kinds. I recall a time our people built a fish dam and had these divers help them. First, they made a drag, long enough to reach across the stream. This they constructed from a grapevine, to which dry brush and small rocks had been tied. This brush dam they stretched across the river, allowing it to nearly touch the bottom, and on each bank were men to pull this drag. The divers went ahead of the drag and frightened the fish from the deep holes, when they naturally moved toward the dam...

On one occasion we were fishing at a place called "Sit-wall-Co" [about three miles upriver from Hopland]. After we had built our dam we began diving ahead of the drag. One of our men went down this time and got caught, but we were quick enough to save him. Many a good diver and swimmer is drowned at this work. During our diving, while we frightened the fish out of the holes, we also caught some. If you want to have fun, try this; it is much more sport than fishing with a rod.

Chilula fish dam on Redwood Creek. Photo courtesy of the Phoebe Apperson Hearst Museum of Anthropology and the Regents of the University of California, #15-297983.

How Eel Lost Its Bones

SUSAN CALLA, SANDRA JERABEK,
AND LOREN BOMMELYN, TOLOWA

At one time Eel had lots of ribs and bones in its body. However, after hundreds of years of going up and down the river each spring to spawn, its bones were eventually worn away. Finally only three ribs were left.

One spring Eel was very tired from fighting the swift upstream current. While resting among the rocks and submerged willow roots, she had an idea. She would try to get Sucker to give her some of his bones, which would make her much stronger and make it easier for her to swim long distances.

She challenged Sucker to a stick game, which he found very amusing, since he was known as the greatest stick player. Sucker found a quiet pool at the edge of the river and began to play with Eel.

Eel insisted they play for bones and ribs. When one lost to the other, the loser had to pull a bone from its body and give it to the winner, who would then push it through its skin and into its own body. Well, we know to this day who won the game, because ever since, no eel has ever been born with a bone in its body!

Eel and salmon cooking on an outdoor grill at the Requa home of Merk Oliver (Yurok), 1991. Photo courtesy of Mark Johnson.

River Eel

BRADLEY MARSHALL, HUPA

Build a fire with manzanita wood and let it burn until you have a bed of red-hot coals. Manzanita wood is important because it gets real hot and won't leave a lot of ash on the eel. Lay the eels out on a metal screen on top of the coals or directly on the coals. Roll them around a couple of times. The way to tell if an eel is done is to wrap a string around it and pull both ends; if the string cuts through cleanly, then the eel is cooked. Once cool, pick up the eels with a fork and hit them with a stick or wipe with your hand to remove the ashes.

Fresh Smelts
Native Cookbook

Smelt (Spirinchus starksi), *also called surf fish and night fish, come in to spawn at night. They are about six to ten inches along.*

20 smelts
Salt
Pepper
Flour
Oil

Wash smelts in running water. Dry and sprinkle with salt and pepper. Roll smelts in flour and sauté in oil on medium heat until golden brown (approximately 5–10 minutes).

Red Soup (An Ocean Soup Pot)

KATHLEEN ROSE SMITH, YOLETAMAL/BODEGA MIWOK AND
MIHILAKAWNA/DRY CREEK POMO

This is more of a recipe of "being" than a recipe for "cooking," since precise measurements and cooking times are not included. To make a successful soup at the ocean requires the presence of family or friends. The important thing is being there and being part of that group experience.

What to bring: bring a pot large enough to feed everyone, with a wire handle suitable for camp cooking. If a fire with burning embers is allowed, cook over this. Otherwise, a camp stove will do. Also bring a current fishing license, fresh water, one or more onions, a large or small can of tomatoes (whole, diced, sliced, or whatever), one or two carrots, one or two stalks of celery, one or two potatoes, and about a cup of red wine. Heat the water in the pot. Meanwhile, chop or dice the vegetables. The rest of the soup depends on your catch of the day, whatever you can fish for legally from rocks, such as bullhead and shellfish, mussels especially. Clean the seafood and chop it up, if necessary. Add to the pot, then add the wine. Simmer until cooked to taste.

After a long day of fishing or gathering shellfish, this meal is absolutely delicious.

Left: Surf fish drying at the beach on sand mounds covered with dried grass. Photo by Beverly Hanly. Right: Gathering fish on the beach at a Tolowa fish camp. Photo by Beverly Hanly.

SHELLFISH and SEAWEED

Foods gathered along the sea's edge were among the delicacies of Native California cuisine. Along the northern coast, seaweed was a popular snack food. Some species of shellfish, such as sea urchins, were eaten raw at the beach, while others, such as barnacles, were roasted or dried. Methods of collecting these foods are quite direct, with abalone posing the greatest challenge. In prehistoric times people used hardwood sticks with flat ends to pry the animals off their rocks. Today, a similar tool made of metal is used, though collecting is strictly regulated by the state of California because of the extreme depletion of red abalone populations.

The famous Pismo clam and those local to the San Francisco Bay are gone now. But they were enjoyed robustly, as were crabs, limpets, sea anemones, mussels (gathered from the ocean, rivers, and lakes), snails, and many other species. Tribes that gathered food at the shore had ways of knowing when harmful bacteria were present in the seawater that would make shellfish toxic, and avoided collecting during these times.

Like other food sources, the abalone harvest was regulated through song and ritual; without the correct songs,

according to writer Greg Sarris, "the tide would get you." And shellfish populations were actively managed through careful harvests. Researcher Rob Baker describes the clam beds in Tomales Bay as a garden cultivated by informed caretakers. By repeatedly culling the larger clams from the beds, Coast Miwoks made sure that young clams had sufficient space to grow.

Shellfish were valued not just for their meat, but also for their shells, which some tribes fashioned into beads and treated as money, particularly dentalia in the northwest and clamshells among the tribes of the central coast. Trade in California was extensive and small items like shell beads traveled far. Multilingual traders moved from one region to the next with coastal trade items in hand: not only shells and finished beads, but also abalone, dried fish, and kelp were taken to inland tribes.

Gathering is best accomplished on a day at the beach with lots of hands to do the work. Spending the day like this serves to reinforce the feeling that Kathleen Rose Smith calls "knowing one's place in the order of things"—the order being nature's, and the surge of the surf being a reminder of a power much greater than one's own.

Mussels. Photo by Frank Magallanes and Althea Edwards.

Mussels

JACQUELYN ROSS, JENNER POMO/COAST MIWOK

Mussels properly gathered are delicious. You can find them in the seafood section of supermarkets, or you can order them in upscale restaurants, often awash with some type of elaborate sauce. For me, simpler is better. We steam the mussels in a big canning pot. Then we protect the table with several layers of newspapers and place the pot of freshly steamed mussels in the middle. With bowls of garlic butter, hot sauce, and French bread on the sidelines, we start our annual mussel feed. Usually, there is not much talk for the first half hour or so, just the sound of empty shells landing on top of each other in a pile.

The mussel season, often beginning in November, is an exciting time. I start and end each visit with a prayer of thanks. As we hunt, we try to be extremely careful in our conduct. The coastline may look like a rough and rugged place, but tidal environments are delicate; each tide-pool area is its own small world. When we go to the ocean, we are visiting many homes, so we are careful where we put our hands and feet; we are careful of what we touch. When gathering mussels, I try to take only a few from each spot, gently, so as not to disturb the others. And I don't expose a place where a big wave could come and knock other mussels off their rock. Many other animals find their shelter in the mussel bed, so it is their home, too.

Gathering Shellfish

DELFINA CUERO, KUMEYAAY

We used to hunt for all kinds of shellfish. We would boil some to eat then. We would clean, wash, and cut the rest and spread them on the rocks to dry in the sun. If we had *si·* (salt), we would put that on and the meat would keep better. We used to get salt down at the southern edge of San Diego Bay.

We used a sharp rock that fitted in your hand with a joint at one end to get abalone off the rocks. We used to search around the rocks at low tide for them. You have to pound the meat of abalone soft with a rock right away. Then you cut it up and set the meat to dry in the sun, just like the other fish. The *xa·lyak* (abalone shell) made food dishes; other smaller shells were used for spoons.

My grandparents used to eat a small white part [the stomach] of the *ci·k·alyap* (starfish), but I never ate them myself. Crabs are good meat too. We ate many things that look ugly but that are good meat. I remember we caught a *xilketa·t* (octopus) a long time ago; it was real ugly, but food. If you dig a hole in the muddy sand with a digging stick and put water in it with an olla, the *ki·xui* (clams) will come up. We ate scallops too. Anything we could take, we ate. We ate *milykama·w* (lobster) and wee little stuff that looked like spiders, real small *ki·tas* (shrimp).

There was a story about the olivella shell; they were babies that fell from the stars. They used to say: When the dipper in the sky [the Big Dipper] gets too full, it is dumped out. Then these small shells fall all around near the ocean. There was more to it but I am not a storyteller and that is all

I can remember. They used to name all the stars and tell stories about them, and explain why the dipper is lying differently in summer and winter.

We caught fish and cleaned them. We took the fins, tail, and head off and used those parts to make a good soup. The eyes, especially, were good for you. I thought they were so ugly that I never cared for them, but I used them to make good soup. I would clean the fish and boil it to eat. When we got a lot, we would cut it all up and dry the meat in the sun for later. We used cactus thorns on a long stick to spear fish. We also made traps out of agave fiber. We put the traps in the ocean, put a piece of rabbit meat in it, and could come back later to get the fish. We made nets out of tall grasses; ropes and nets were made of agave too. We had other ways to catch fish too, but I don't remember them all. The women made small nets and the men made big ones. I can remember the old timers' talk about making *kayus* (boat) out of *tamu•* (reeds). They would weave them so tightly that the water could not get through.

Kathleen Rose Smith gathering turban snails and other shellfish at low tide in Marin County. Photo by Beverly R. Ortiz.

The Origin of Abalone

GLADYS NOMLAND

A girl came from the south—came and stood a long way off from a man. He wanted to get her because she was covered with Indian money. He said to his grandmother, "How am I going to get that woman?" His grandmother said, "Sing a song to her and she will come to you." So the grandmother gave him a song and he sang it to the woman. His grandmother told him that he must be out hunting when the girl came.

One day the grandmother heard shells on a dress and saw the girl coming. She shone all over with the abalone shell, she looked just like a rainbow. Then the man came home dressed in finery, dressed just like a hummingbird. He saw the girl was old and ugly, so he turned his back on her. She went away, went to the north, and his grandmother told the boy he did very wrong. The girl went a short distance and came to a creek where she changed back to a beautiful young woman. He saw her and followed her again. She went on and on. She stopped at Klamath River and he followed and caught up with her there on the left side of the river.

He wanted her to go back with him, but she said no. He said he would cut her up so that she would never be pretty again. She would not go back, so he cut her. He left then, and she went to Trinidad and washed the blood, and her body came back beautiful again. That man saw her again and he wanted to get her. She came toward him and told him that she would not go back with him but that she would always leave abalone shell for him to see so that he should not come after her again. Then she cried and sang a song.

That love song is the oldest song the Bear River people have. After she came back to her family, her sister said, "What happened to you?" She said, "I've been all cut up. I'll never follow another man." The tiny abalone shells are the oldest girl's body. When she arrived home south, the man was already there. She would not marry him, but he stayed there with her and this is why abalone money stays at Trinidad, and that is the reason women do not follow men but have the men follow the women. Abalone is found only where that girl stopped to swim when she traveled, and it is always rough, because she was all cut up by that man.

Abalone and seaweed at Westport Union Landing, 1981.
Photo by Scott M. Patterson.

Abalone: A Precious Gift

KATHLEEN ROSE SMITH, YOLETAMAL/BODEGA MIWOK AND
MIHILAKAWNA/DRY CREEK POMO

On the first day of April the pilgrimage will continue. Once again dark figures will emerge out of the misty fog and move slowly to the sea. Men dressed head to toe in black will awkwardly descend, backward, into the icy surf, float a short distance on the ocean surface, then disappear. After what seems a long, long time, each will once more appear, bringing with him, if blessed with good fortune, a precious treasure only the sea can give. Abalone.

Of course, the quest for abalone did not always begin on April Fool's Day. This is a comparatively recent occurrence initiated by the fishing regulations of the state of California. Abalone, arguably the most delectable of the foods of my people, has long been eaten by California's coastal and Channel Island Indians. When it was realized that restaurants would pay high prices for abalone, a new industry was created, as was the need to control the excesses of modern commerce.

Unlike during the days when abalone were gathered by small, hardy groups of individuals to feed their own families and friends, these creatures, like so many of the seafood delicacies (such as turban snails and sea urchins), now need to be protected from extinction at the hands of people whose motivation for gathering is dollars alone.

During my childhood, abalone could be picked off the rocks at low tide. Today, this is rarely so. Men and women, such as Aunt Josie (Josephine Santos Wright), would search for abalone armed with a burlap sack and a handmade prying tool—a pointed stick, tire iron, or anything else with which they could carefully remove the abalone without cutting its flesh. They would dress as warmly as they could, wearing woolen sweaters, long johns under loose-fitting cotton duck pants, and rubber-soled, canvas shoes. All this helped to shield them against the chilly waves, slippery rocks, and modern codes of social propriety. (Their own ancestors had plied these same icy waters with no clothes whatsoever.) Bemused white people thought they were fanatical or nuts.

Then the French ocean explorer Jacques Cousteau invented the wet suit, and this changed the method of abalone gathering. Because of the wet suit, the risk of drowning due to hypothermia was considerably reduced for those who had not grown up swimming in northern California's freezing ocean. True, one still has to be hardy and have strong lungs to dive into fifteen feet or so of buoyant sea water, aided only by lead weights around the waist.

Removing abalone from the rocks on the ocean floor is actually easier than taking them from the tidal zone, according to my nephew Steve Smith. They don't hold on as strongly to the rocks below the constant wave action.

There are many ways to prepare abalone, truly one of the world's finest gourmet foods. The best I have tasted was prepared by Steve. He was kind enough to allow me to present it and other remembrances here. Now in his early forties, Steve, like all of his people, has spent a lifetime fishing and enjoying the ocean: "Just being at the ocean is so relaxing; remembering the old times with Dad (Russell Smith), Uncle Manuel (Manuel Cordova), and Grandpa (Steven Smith, Jr.) makes it all worth it [the danger and cold]. It's renewing and

makes the challenge of commuting and work less stressful just to remember those times."

They would make a fire on the beach to dry off. "Sometimes," Steve said, "Uncle Manuel and Grandpa would wait until there was only a bed of coals left, then place an 'ab' on the coals, face down, still in its shell, and cover the abalone with coals and rocks." Later, they would dig the cooked abalone out. The shell and guts would be burned off. Then they trimmed off all the charcoal and ate the chewy meat. "It was delicious." I, too, remember having abalone cooked this way on the beach when I was a youngster.

Steve also told about someone he met who was a friend of my grandfather and great-uncles (the Smith brothers of Bodega Bay, who started the modern Sonoma County fishing industry). The friend said that the Smith brothers would make jerky out of abalone at great-grandfather Bill Smith's ranch at the bay. (Great-grandmother Rosalie Charles Smith had already died by this time.) Perhaps some of my cousins that lived at the bay remember this, too.

Above: Sonoma coast, spring 2000. Photo by Beverly R. Ortiz.
Inset: Brothers Bruce and Steven Smith (left and middle) with their uncle, Doug Smith (all Dry Creek Pomo/Bodega Miwok), preparing to dive for abalone along the Sonoma coast. Photo by Beverly R. Ortiz.

Top, left to right: Freshly shucked abalone being prepared for a meal during a gathering of the extended family of Lucy and Steven Smith; Doug Smith removing abalone from the shell; Doug Smith slicing abalone. Bottom, left to right: Abalone soaking in a milk and egg mixture; abalone being breaded; breaded abalone frying in a cast-iron skillet. Photos by Beverly R. Ortiz.

Steve Smith's Breaded Abalone

KATHLEEN ROSE SMITH, YOLETAMAL/BODEGA MIWOK AND MIHILAKAWNA/DRY CREEK POMO

Remove abalone from shell and clean. (If you are interested, carefully run the guts between your fingers, as sometimes there is a pearl inside. It will be the same colors as the shell.)

Next, slice cleaned abalone lengthwise, one-quarter to three-eighths of an inch thick. Have ready: milk, two eggs, cracker crumbs, olive oil, dry white wine, and a wok.

Pound slices with a flat, smooth weight, such as a mallet or the iron used to pry abalone from the rock. (Check regulations with California State Department of Fish and Game if unfamiliar with this term. The measurements and other specifications regarding what to use when removing abalone from the rocks are strictly regulated.) Pound two or more times, until the abalone's texture is about to tear. Steve also includes the "foot" (that part that attaches to the rock) in his slices. Trim off and save the edges for chowder or fish bait. The edges are black, so it's easy to see and remove them. If using for chowder, scrape the black off. All of this can be frozen to use later.

Soak slices in a mixture of milk, eggs, and white wine. Use enough soaking mixture to cover all slices. For two abalones, use one and a half cups of milk and two eggs, beaten together. Add one-third to one-half cup of dry white wine.

Grind up enough soda crackers in a blender to coat abalone slices. Remove slices from soaking mixture.

Heat wok to 375-400°. Use enough olive oil to fry abalone slices.

Roll slices in cracker crumbs, coating them completely. Then carefully place them into the hot oil. To test if the oil is hot enough, put a small amount of the cracker crumbs in the wok. When it's the right heat, the crumbs will bubble.

Turn abalone slices once. Cook each side 35 to 40 seconds.

Season abalone with fresh lemon juice, if desired. Serve with steamed rice and fresh garden salad. And, if you are lucky enough to have some, decant and serve a bottle of my brother Bill's Pomo Ridge Dry Creek Valley Chardonnay for a meal you will remember for a long time.

Abalone Chowder
Native Cookbook

2 cups minced or chopped abalone	3 cups milk
Water	2 tablespoons flour
3 slices bacon, diced	1 tablespoon butter
1 cup onion, chopped	1 teaspoon celery salt
3 potatoes, peeled and diced	
2 cups canned whole kernel corn, drained	

Drain abalone; if using canned abalone, save the liquid and add enough water to make 1 cup. Cook bacon until crisp; add onions and cook until tender. Add potatoes, water, and abalone liquid; cover and simmer gently until potatoes are tender. Add corn and milk. Blend flour and butter together and stir into soup. Cook slowly until mixture thickens slightly, stirring constantly but gently. Add seasonings and abalone, simmer 5 minutes. Top with croutons or cracker crumbs and serve piping hot.

Ingeniously Roasted Barnacles
ROBERT E. GREENGO

One of the most ingenious methods of procuring any shellfish was practiced by the Pomo, who...would at low tide build a fire over a bed of barnacles living on the rocks...This was kept going, cooking the barnacles, until the incoming tide extinguished the fire and cooled the meal, which was eaten the next day.

Barbecued Clams
Native Cookbook

2 to 3 dozen clams, or
4 dozen steamer clams, shucked
8 to 10 wooden skewers, soaked in water
Sardine oil, or melted butter
½ to 1 cup alder, apple, or hickory wood chips, soaked in
    water for at least 30 minutes

Thread 4 to 6 clams on each skewer. Brush with oil. Prepare barbecue grill. Sprinkle flavored wood chips over hot coals. Grill clams for 3 to 8 minutes, depending on their size. Turn and baste once with oil. Serve with additional oil or butter for dipping.

Seaweed Season
HILLARY RENICK, FORT BRAGG POMO/PAVIOTSO PAIUTE

I grew up in a traditional household (something I did not fully understand until I moved to Washington, D.C., to attend college). We always had a lot of Indian food, since my grandpa and dad had friends and relations all over Indian Country. If there were something that we wanted, we would trade another Indian for it.

Every spring we would go to my grandfather's seaweed rock, just north of Fort Bragg. There he knew of a spot where seaweed came out "early," which was usually late February or early March. In the spring and early summer there would be other Indians, from the interior, who would come and camp on our beaches. Indians from Laytonville, Coyote Valley, Covelo, Lake County, and the Sacramento Valley would camp with their families on the beaches between Fort Bragg and Juan Creek. I remember having lots of aunts and uncles at our camp at Ten Mile.

The seaweed is dried on sheets on the beach or any other flat surface. After drying both sides, it is quite a bit lighter! So if you're on a steep beach, you won't have to lug a heavy load up the trail. You can put the seaweed in soup or fry it and put it in a tortilla (*tup tup* is the Pomo word for tortilla bread). Other seafood is also taken home to cook, but if there is a camp, the surf fish (sometimes you catch perch or salmon too) can be cooked up for dinner.

Mabel McKay (Pomo) picking seaweed, Sonoma County coast, 1982. Photo by Scott M. Patterson.

Harvesting, Storing, and Preparing Seaweed

HILLARY RENICK, FORT BRAGG POMO/PAVIOTSO PAIUTE

Take the seaweed from the rocks, making sure that it is in a good area (an area that is not too populated). It's best to get the seaweed from the ocean side of the rocks, since there will be less sand. If you want, rinse it in the surf. It's best to carry it in a "breathable" container, such as a potato sack or pillowcase; this will allow the water to drain out and will prevent mold. Once you are home or back at camp (the same day), you must dry it. Take an old sheet and spread it on a flat surface (any surface will do: lawn, table, etc.). Lay the seaweed out in strips that are thin enough for you to see its greenish tint. Ideal weather conditions would be sunny with a little breeze. Let it dry until the only noticeably wet part is on the bottom. You will notice that when dried it will become darker and lighter in spots. Turn the strips over and dry the other side. It's best to stay close during this part, since the strips will be very light and the wind could pick up. When the seaweed is done, put it in a pillowcase and store in a dry area. It will last for more than a year.

When you are ready for a taste, get a frying pan and pour in about a half-inch of your favorite cooking oil (the healthier, the better). Set the burner on just-below-medium (on my stove, it's 4.5). When the oil is ready, place strips of seaweed in the pan. Turn them after about two minutes and cook the other side for about one minute. Have a plate on the side ready to drain the oil. Line the plate with two or three paper towels and press the grease out. The seaweed should be sparkly, light, and translucent. The perfect strip will melt in your mouth. If your first batch doesn't come out like this, try again. Warm up some *tup tup*, place the cooked seaweed inside, and enjoy.

Seaweed Broth

Native Cookbook

Large bunch of dried seaweed
5 cups water

Harvest and dry seaweed in advance—it needs to be dried in hot sun until brittle. Blend seaweed in blender until powdery. Add water to make broth for soup and steep for flavor. Serve warm—add flour dumplings if desired.

Opposite page, top: The late Milton "Bun" Lucas (Kashaya Pomo/Coast Miwok) gathering seaweed in a whole-shoot willow basket he made, 1991. Bottom, left: Seaweed during a gathering trip with Lucas, 1988; right, seaweed drying on Kathleen Rose Smith's cloth utel, *2000. Photos by Beverly R. Ortiz.*

MEAT

A stereotypical image of the Native American man is that of a hunter who lived by his wits and his keen knowledge of the habits and habitats of countless animal species. The image is not entirely erroneous—a hunter needs skill, daring, and know-how—but it seems also a reflection of the heroic symbolism of meat in people's lives. Meat is the ultimate source of protein and fat, an important sustenance highly prized and joyfully received, and sometimes highly circumscribed by ritual prohibitions. Even today, Native peoples all over California—for example, northwestern dancers preparing for a ceremonial cycle—will, in order to purify their spirits, refrain from eating meat and some other foods. Traditionally, hunting itself often required proper spiritual preparation and, afterwards, the proper prayers of thanks.

Both large and small game were and are taken by Native Californians—with rifles, arrows, clubs, decoys, nets, traps, slings, snares, pits, fire drives, spears, sticks, and knives. Large animals, like elk, deer, sea lions, and mountain sheep, were difficult to hunt, and their meat was proportionally esteemed. The meat from these animals was often shared among community members according to cultural rules. But perhaps because they were more plentiful, the little critters, like chipmunks, squirrels, birds, and wood rats, made up a larger part of the diet. Birds and their eggs were much loved; Patrick Orozco (Ohlone) recalls eating his grand-

mother's goose-and-seagull-egg pudding, a recipe that has unfortunately been lost to time. Certain animals were never eaten, such as grizzly bears. This may have been because of their likeness to humans, as well as the fact that they were known to eat human beings at times. Today, the state of California imposes legal taboos on hunting that don't always match tribal laws, as in 1999, when the state brought poaching charges against a Yurok man for hunting and killing two elk in Redwood National Park (he was fined $125 and given three years probation).

Small mammals were typically pounded and roasted, bones included. In general, meat was eaten freshly cooked, or dried over the course of one to two weeks to prevent the growth of mold and bacteria. In southern California, the Cahuilla soaked and boiled their meat jerky, while the Atsugewi, in northeastern California, made sausage by filling a wildcat paunch. Pit or earth ovens were another method, one that is still popular: a deep hole is dug and lined with rocks, a fire is lit, and eventually the meat (wrapped in leaves in the old days, or sometimes in soaked burlap or aluminum foil today) is placed inside and cooked for twelve to twenty-four hours.

As Richard Bugbee (Payoomkawichum) relates, acorns may have been the staple food of many California tribes, but meat was the "main" food. Often served with acorn dishes, meat holds great nutritional, gastronomic, and ritual importance in the lives of California Indians.

Western sage grouse hen. Photo by Frank Magallanes and Althea Edwards.

When Meat Came from Animals

RICHARD BUGBEE, PAYOOMKAWICHUM

Long ago, food was medicine to maintain the body. Food was nourishing, not harmful. Food provided all the nutrients needed by the body; it was not loaded with carcinogens and chemical preservatives. People ate healthy food, mostly lean wild meat and staple plant foods like acorns, mesquite, pine nuts, and agave.

Tribes had social restrictions on avoiding certain foods at certain times. Men had food restrictions before ceremonies and women had monthly restrictions of meat, fat, and salt. These food restrictions contributed to the balanced, healthy lifestyle of the tribe by keeping each member, as well as the whole community, healthy. In some communities, young bachelors couldn't eat anything they killed during the hunt, but were instead required to give it to the elders.

While reviewing a San Diego Museum of Man pamphlet I had edited for the Native American Advisory Council for California State Parks, Clarence Brown, a Kumeyaay elder, corrected me regarding the main food of the Kumeyaay. He edited the pamphlet to emphasize that the "main food" of the Kumeyaay was not acorns, but meat. Acorns were the "staple"—the side dish for every meal, like potatoes, beans, or rice.

Growing up in my family, we always had fresh wild meat, like rabbit, dove, quail, duck, fish, shellfish, and, sometimes, fresh deer meat, mainly brought to the table by my grandfather or my uncle Max. The best hunter of my family was my grandfather's brother, Max Peters from Pauma, who would disappear for a couple of days up on Mt. Palomar, Pa'áa'aw.

We knew when he was home because we would see a deer carcass hanging from the porch of his trailer.

My grandfather, John Peters, always provided us with fresh meat, whether it was wild rabbits, birds, deer, or domesticated cattle that he had raised. My grandfather was one of the last Indian vaqueros. Even in his later years he would always have a few head of cattle to provide fresh meat for us as the wild game became scarce. So I always knew the steer before it was on the table.

Every year my grandfather would make me a set of chaps and a vest from the hide of a deer he had hunted. I would always look to find the bullet hole. I remember that we ate every part of the deer, even its face. I always had to have my mother pull the meat off, because it would stare at me when I tried.

My grandfather took me on my first hunting trip when I was about six years old. We went to Kearny Mesa, a big, flat field with sagebrush. Today it is a commercial suburban sprawl. I was excited when my grandfather got a rabbit in the sights of his rifle. But when he shot the rabbit I started crying and told him he had killed Peter Cottontail. When we got home it was okay, because my mother cooked him, I ate him, and it was good.

In the old days different meats were used for protein. *Qáwla*, wood rat, was one of the favorite animal foods. Fish were also part of the diet; freshwater and saltwater fish, as well as shellfish, were valuable for their nutrients and added variety to the daily diet. Also providing valuable protein were insects and grubs. Small animal bones were ground up and added to foods for needed calcium, and large animal bones were split and the marrow used for its nutritional value and taste.

Men had rabbit sticks for hunting. Young boys were given small sticks, and these sticks got bigger as the boys turned to men. Giant rabbit nets were made of dogbane fiber for communal rabbit hunts. Some of the nets were more than four feet high and seventy feet long. The community would work together to herd the rabbits into the giant net stretched across a field.

The last recorded rabbit hunt in San Diego took place on Coronado in the early 1900s. The women, wrapped in rabbit-skin blankets, made campfires on the beach, and the men hunted rabbits with their rabbit sticks. Noticing that they had a considerable non-Indian audience, the men started showing off by abandoning the rabbit sticks and catching the rabbits by outrunning them.

Growing up, I always knew where animal meat came from. While teaching at the Museum of Man, I noticed that the children associated meat with the cellophane and styrofoam packaging in the supermarket, not the actual animal. Maybe we are getting too far away from giving thanks for the animals and plants that nourish us, as they are no longer recognizable.

Blacktail deer, Yosemite. Photo by Frank Magallanes and Althea Edwards.

Rabbit Liver with Watercress

SYLVIA ROSS, CHUKCHANSI,
AND MARGARET VALDEZ, YOWLUMNI

Livers from 3 rabbits or hares, about 1 pound
1 to 2 tablespoons cooking oil
½ cup finely chopped onion
2 cups finely chopped watercress
1 teaspoon salt

Slowly sauté rabbit livers in skillet. Do not let brown. Do not season before cooking, but after cooking rinse, drain, and sprinkle with salt. Let meat cool. After the meat is cooled, blend in a food processor (or run through a manual kitchen grinder) with fresh onion and watercress. Chill the mixture. Serve on tortillas or crackers. (Note: this dish does not freeze well. Keep refrigerated and only prepare what can be eaten within two days.)

Yokuts pigeon snare ambush. Photo courtesy of the Phoebe Apperson Hearst Museum of Anthropology and the Regents of the University of California, #15-2495.

Roasted Wood Rats

JUSTIN FARMER, IPAI

As a child, I had the good fortune to associate quite a bit with my cousin Dave Osuna, our apple ranch foreman. Dave lived five days a week in a house on our ranch and two days at his house on the Santa Ysabel reservation. When asked about his favorite meal, Dave Osuna would salivate a bit and then describe hunting and roasting tender young wood rats. These were smaller than a cottontail rabbit and lived in nests of piled-up sticks, wood chips, dried grass, leaves, or anything else that makes a house a home. To coax them out of their nests, Dave set fire to the whole mess. He then solemnly laid them to rest with a throwing stick, a rock, an arrow, or any other device known to ancient man. The wood was allowed to burn down to coals and the deceased animal was placed directly on the live coals with all body parts intact. It was turned several times but generally allowed to roast down to what resembled a badly charred piece of jerky, sans hair or any other recognizable part. After the fire died away, the morsel was retrieved from the ashes, its tail and its teeth discarded, and the remainder, including bones, pounded until it was about the thickness and texture of a dark brown tortilla.

Hunting with Mom

DEBRA UTACIA KROL, SALINAN/ESSELEN

Growing up in San Lucas, I rarely ate red meats. Instead, we relied on home-grown vegetables, beans, tortillas, rice, the occasional acorn treat, and game meats. My mom, Mary Larson Bishop, and grandfather, Ed Bracisco, regularly hunted for our table. I grew up on venison, rabbit, quail, and dove; I think that's why, up to now, our family hasn't suffered so badly from the diabetes epidemic ravaging Indian Country.

Mom recently told me a story about a time when she had to compete with other species at the top of the California food chain for venison stew. In 1960, she traveled to the top of the Los Burros Ridge, above Plaskett Creek along the Monterey County coastline. Arriving ahead of the rest of her party, she took out her reliable single-shot .30-30 rifle and padded into the forest floor. She quickly found a buck willing to give himself up for the consumption of human people and made a quick, clean kill.

Finding the buck too heavy to haul, Mom butchered him on the spot, wrapped half the carcass, and hung it high to discourage predators, and wrapped the other half and hauled it back to the deer camp. After slinging this half in another tree, Mom washed up, ate dinner, and retired to her bunk on top of her old Chevy panel truck.

The next morning dawned cold and foggy, a typical California coast morning. Mom prepared and drank her coffee and ate breakfast as the sun rose to warm the treetops over the Santa Lucia Range. Every now and then, her nose caught a whiff of something rotten, like a rotted animal.

Just then her hunting buddies, Cliff Mead and his son, arrived. Cliff jumped from his vehicle, took one look at the tracks surrounding Mom's encampment, and exclaimed, "Mary, didn't you see the mountain lion?"

"What mountain lion?" asked Mom.

"The mountain lion that's been stalking you." Cliff showed her the tracks, and sure enough, a cougar had been circling her camp, hoping for his or her share of Mom's catch. Naturally, the stench came from the lion.

In the old days, the People relied on drying to preserve meats and fish. They would prepare the meat by cutting small strips from the carcass, then hanging the strips up to dry. How they kept bugs off, nobody knows anymore.

In more modern times, people like our grandfather sprinkled salt and pepper on the meat strips and hung them on the metal clothesline out back of our tidy little house in San Lucas. Somehow, the bugs never invaded those tasty venison snacks.

Today, my dad, Warren, uses the same recipe to prepare venison jerky; however, he uses a jerky box handcrafted with a wooden frame and window screen to keep flies and other insects off his gourmet creations. Some people marinate their meat in wine, teriyaki sauce, or other such concoctions, but my family sticks by the tried-and-true method.

My daughter Melissa uses one of those "high-tech" home dehydrators to prepare venison and elk jerky. Another jerky drying trick that I've never used but understand works is to arrange the meat on a cookie tray and place it in a 100° oven for 24 hours or until the meat is completely dry.

In any case, it's vital to allow the meat to dry completely; otherwise, you will have spoilage.

Left: Fernando Librado (Chumash) scraping an arrow shaft with a broken clamshell to bring it to uniform size before straightening it on a stone. Right, top: Librado removing branches from an arrow shaft. Above: Steam-heating an ironwood stick before bending it to make a bow. All photos c. 1912 by Gerald Cassidy, courtesy of the Braun Research Library, Autry National Center #P666, #P675, #P673.

Porcupine

WILLIAM SIMMONS

George Peconom and Ron Morales [Honey Lake Maidu] hunted porcupine here [at Ch'onoim yamanim, literally Porcupine Mountain, northeast of Susanville] among the small oaks. Although Morales knows that the Maidu once used porcupine quills for combs and headbands, he hunted them only for food.

To cook the porcupine, they would first dig a hole approximately four feet wide and four feet deep. Then they would gather and burn hardwood and mahogany in the hole for several hours until they had built a bed of glowing coals. Next they would cut the guts out and put a wire through the porcupine, place it over the coals, and singe off the quills. Then they would scrape the singed quills with a piece of wood, cover the coals with lava rocks, wrap the porcupine with a piece of burlap sacking, and place it on top of the heated rocks. The final step was to cover the pit tightly with pieces of wood and then cover the wood with loose earth to retain the heat while the porcupine cooked for eight to ten hours. They cooked woodchucks, deer, pronghorn, and other game by the same method. [Ron Morales and others] currently cook meat this way at the annual Bear Dance ceremony.

Quail and Doves

KENNETH M. STEWART

The Mojave roasted quail and doves in earth ovens (hapaug). The process was described as follows: "They'd build a fire and burn the feathers up. Then they bake him under hot ashes. Put the bird right in the fire, and work around with a stick until the feathers are burnt up. Then they took out the guts and baked it. Men did it."

Lake Turtles

SAMUEL A. BARRETT

The turtle was caught [by the Pomo] and used as food. About Clear Lake the turtles came out to sun themselves at certain places on the flattened-down stems along the strip of tule which fringes the shore. A net was placed just under the surface of the water at such a point. Later, when several turtles had congregated, they were suddenly startled and caused to dive. In their endeavors to escape they became entangled in the net.

A turtle may be placed directly in the fire. As soon as the shell cracks open, the meat is taken out and placed on the coals to broil. In another method the turtle is placed in the hot ashes to bake. This is a much slower process but when the baking is completed the shell is cracked open and the meat is ready to eat.

Red-eared slider turtle (not native to California), La Canada. Photo by Frank Magallanes and Althea Edwards.

in a chert arrowhead speckled with
    quartz
i have seen our grandfathers
along a stream east of the valley
lancing salmon and deer
                    —*William Oandasan, Yuki*

Hupa deer hunter. Photo courtesy of The Field Museum, #CSA9562.
Opposite page: The late Wayne Marufo (Kashaya Pomo) pit-roasting
deer meat. Photo by Beverly R. Ortiz.

Venison Casserole

JOSEPHINE PETERS, KARUK/SHASTA/ABENAKE

Start with 4 cups venison, cubed into small pieces and rolled in flour. Put two tablespoons of lard in a skillet. Add venison and brown. When browned add 1½ cups water. Add 2 tablespoons chopped onion and season to taste with salt and pepper. Simmer until venison is tender.

Add two cups acorn soup (see Acorn chapter, p. 97) and one cup mushrooms chopped into small pieces. Simmer another 15 minutes.

Pour mixture into 12 x 8 inch baking dish.

Mix 1½ cups flour, ½ cup corn meal, a pinch of salt, 1 teaspoon baking powder, 1 tablespoon melted lard, and ¾ cup water into a dough. On a floured board pat dough out flat, about ½ inch thick, to fit on top of the venison mixture. Bake at 350° until bread top is done.

John Olivera (Miwok), left, and Andrew George (Pit River) use paddles to remove bones and stir a stew made from meat cooked in an earth oven at the Lassen Yah-Monee Maidu Bear Dance, near Susanville, June 9, 2007. Photo by Sara-Larus Tolley.

Bodega Bay Acorn Beef Stew

DAVID W. PERI, BODEGA MIWOK

You'll need 1½ to 2 pounds of stewing beef (or boneless steak if you can afford it; the meat should be in one single piece, not cut up), and two or three medium-sized white or red potatoes. Baking potatoes can also be used. The white or red ones will not mush up like the baking ones will. However, in this case it's more a matter of texture than taste as to which ones you use. You will also need ½ to ¾ cup of finely ground acorn meal. Have salt and pepper handy as well.

Place the meat whole in a frying pan. One of the old-fashioned, heavy metal ones does the best. You will need a pan slightly larger than the piece of meat. Add water to about ¼ inch above the meat. Dice the potatoes and place them around the meat. Cover the pan with a lid and simmer very, very slowly. When the meat begins to fall apart, it's done. In any event, simmer it until it's very tender. Next, remove the meat and cut into small pieces. While you are cutting the meat, keep the heat and the lid on the pan. Put the meat back into the pan and slowly stir in the acorn meal, letting it cook for about one minute with the lid off. Add salt and pepper to your taste, and stir slowly once more. It's now ready. Serve it on toasted English muffins. If you've done everything right, it will be delicious.

Roasted Meat with Bay and Sage

SYLVIA ROSS, CHUKCHANSI, AND MARGARET VALDEZ, YOWLUMNI

Fresh or thawed leg or shoulder of deer, antelope, or elk
½ cup dried, wild-grown sage
4 bay leaves, fresh or dried
Cooking oil or non-stick spray
Salt and pepper to taste
Honey

Wash meat, pat dry. Cut slits about one inch deep and one inch apart in the meat to be roasted. Insert bay leaf into each cut. Lightly brush meat with oil. Crush dry sage, salt, and pepper together until well blended. Dust oiled meat on all sides with mixture. Wrap meat in aluminum foil or roasting paper and bake at low temperature. Allow at least 30 minutes per pound at 300°. Fifteen minutes before it's done, open foil, brush with warmed honey, and increase temperature to 375° to glaze meat. This basic recipe can also be baked in an outdoor grill or boned and cooked in a large slow-cooker. (Note: remove bay leaves before serving.)

Dose!

DARRYL BABE WILSON (SUL'MA'EJOTE), ITAMI'IS/AW'TE

(I was six years old, hunting with my daddy in Cayton Canyon.)

Soft the black night, thick. The dancing flames painted the face of Daddy an orange mask of deep shadows.

"Quiet, Son, make no noise until our job is done."

A black sky made white with stars watched our movements. From the distant shadows of trees *suka'how* (owl) called. From beyond the black forest below us, *suka'how* answered.

Fire danced. Sparks rained skyward as Daddy sprinkled "medicine" upon the rocks glowing deep. Scorched sage-blossom perfume swept up my nose and pierced my brain. We reached out and "raked" the smoke into our spirits.

Soon, we nestled under the hay in the old barn, moldy, yellow, dusty. Camouflage.

Daddy whispered, "Breathe deep, remain quiet" (a hunter cleansing).

"Rest. *Loqmim* (at the silver of first light), we hunt."

"Now, *tosaqjami* (dream). Call *dose* (deer). See *dose* tonight as you will see it *ameja'ji* (in the light of sun)."

Resting under the hay, I did not rest. I thought there might be a big rattlesnake somewhere nearby, inching ever nearer, silently...

Loqmim. Carefully, we moved through the huge pines. Darkness was all around us, a velvet and black blanket that we could touch yet walk through.

Silver-gray was now upon the horizon. *Suka'how* called again. We stopped, rubbed the leaves and berries of skunk brush between our hands, then all over our clothing, faces, and hair.

"Daddy, we smell like *ha'yana* (skunk)!"

Silently (hunter style, without bending a branch or turning a leaf), we melted into the thick darkness of the forest near the lake and took our position.

Motionless. No cloud of breath. Long we waited. Long and silently we waited. Long and silently and forever.

My body was cramped. My head was aching. My heart was gripped in a vice.

Then!

Daddy tensed. He softly whispered, *"dose..."*

(The urgency in Daddy's voice was a command of several very important things. It meant for me to be quiet, like stone. It meant that the deer we were dreaming of and waiting for had arrived. It meant that I must use all of my hunting power to remain silent—that we were within reach of our quarry. It meant that now the family would eat, and if

Deer's head with eyes dug out and nose closed so it would not know who killed him, Humboldt County, 1907. Photograph by Pliny E. Goddard, courtesy of the Phoebe Apperson Hearst Museum of Anthropology and the Regents of the University of California, #15-4284.

I made a noise, if I breathed, if I in any manner "spooked" the deer and they took flight, I would be responsible for our family having nothing.)

Daddy had the rifle already aimed at his "target." He was set.

Then, my heart leaped and I almost fainted!

There! Almost at the end of Daddy's gun barrel, the *dose* of my dreams! Motionless it stood, as if made from the leaves of the quiet forest.

A small breath of steam came from its nostrils.

It did not blink, it listened.

My spirit screamed, "Shoot, Daddy, shoot!"

Dose peered in all directions, vanished.

Confusion and panic reigned within my being! I remained motionless...

As if by magic, another *dose* appeared—exactly as in my dream, again!

"Shoot!" cried my tormented spirit, again and again.

Many *dose* passed, one hesitating after the other, not breaking a branch.

I had given up on Daddy ever shooting because my entire being, clear to the center of my spirit, was aching with cramps.

"Boom!"

It'ayas (early light) shattered like ice upon a lake in late spring, struck with a heavy stone, splashing. Silence was replaced with Thunder, and acid smoke from the gunpowder filled the air.

"Boom" knocked me back into the thick brush, almost unconscious. Numb from waiting, numb from the report, numb from the fright of seeing the *dose* of my dream,

I lay in the brush dazed, as if I were wounded, not the *dose*.

By the time I recovered, Daddy had opened the *dose*, and steam and a salty smell spewed forth, and blood was upon his hands and upon the earth.

Shivering with fright I saw the painful glitter of blue light, the light of death in the eyes of *dose*. Eyes that only a moment ago could see the whole world shining, now maybe saw shadows of memories only. Upriver, to the south, *ma'ka'da* (coyote) forlornly yipped and howled to a departing night.

My spirit, numb no longer, trembled. My stomach shook. Silently, I cried for *dose*.

As is the custom of our people, Daddy took out the purple liver from the mounds of entrails, cut off a small piece for me and one for himself, and, after calling upon

Quon (the Great power that holds earth just close enough to sun for life to be in abundance) to forgive the injury to the family of the deer and the injury to the silence of morning, he licked the blood from the liver; then, in ceremony, ate it, for now his family could eat also.

I looked at the liver, tasted the fresh blood, and in the manner of all my Grandfathers, put it in my mouth; a warm, sharp taste that I still remember, the soft flesh hesitating for a long moment in my throat before "squiggling" down.

On the way home we stopped to rest. Daddy saw my tears.

"Why do you cry, Son?"

(Trembling...) "'Cause of... *dose*..." A pat on the head.

"There are many things you must learn.

"As hunters we must kill so our family will live. All of nature knows of this. In this manner also, the hunter must obey all of the laws of nature.

"In a herd, the first *dose* is always the leader, strong, young. Do not kill this one. It is in nature that the old ones follow last. This is because the last one is the one ready to be taken, its life has been lived.

"*Maya'ki, piriki, merak'me'ta* (wolf, grizzly bear, mountain lion) know of this. They wait beside the trail as we did. When the last *dose* passes, they spring, just as we did this morning.

"Worry no more, Son.

"It is a great law that you have obeyed. *L'hepta* (let's go). Our family is waiting."

Daddy carried the *dose* homeward on his shoulders. I walked behind carrying the rifle and the knife, feeling very important.

And somehow I knew that I had just taken a big step towards becoming *it'jati'wa* (a genuine man).

(Arriving home just an hour after sunup, we created some excitement bringing home a big *dose*—even the dogs jumped up and down. They were dreaming about bones, I bet. And I think *ha'yana* and *ma'ka'da* got the guts down near the lake.)

VEGETABLES

Bulbs, corms, rhizomes, taproots, and tubers, as well as the leaves and stems of many plant species, were and still are used and enjoyed by Native Californians. Historically and today, Native Californians have attuned themselves to seasonal gathering cycles for green vegetables such as succulent clover (the Sierra Mewuk relished eight different varieties), prickly pear cactus pads, nettles, and watercress. In spring, Sage LaPena (Wintu) gathers miner's lettuce (also known as Indian lettuce) to eat raw in salads. Also in spring, Monique Sonoquie (Chumash) wades through marshes to pick cattails, separating the outer green leaves and pulling out the inner white core. Because cattails are very absorbent, it is especially important to gather them from unpolluted sites. Carbohydrate-rich "Indian potatoes"—a general term used by many Native Californians to refer to the underground stems of various bulbs, corms, tubers, tuberous roots, and rhizomes—complement the seasonal greens.

Vegetable sources of protein and carbohydrates were incredibly diverse in California, particularly before ranching and invasive plant species were introduced to the state. Most plant foods were prepared and consumed simply and in conjunction with other foods. Often eaten raw, fresh greens were also sometimes cooked in baskets, using large, heated stones to boil the cooking water, or steamed in earth ovens with other foods. Fresh and dried leaves were often boiled or steeped to make teas. Wild onion leaves were picked and salted and added to acorn mush for flavor. In southern California, Spanish bayonet was an important vegetable staple; the young basal stalks were steamed in earth ovens. Agave, too, was a boon for the southern peoples. Gathering it was once considered the work of men and boys; it was roasted on site in a pit filled with leaves and grass, and while it cooked the men shared stories with the boys and taught them dances and songs.

This chapter focuses on wild plant foods, but the tribes of the Colorado River area and possibly some neighboring groups as well have long practiced varying degrees of agriculture, raising aboriginal varieties of corn, gourds, sunflowers, pumpkins, tepary beans, melons, and, after contact with Europeans, many other crops, including wheat and cowpeas. And Native Californians continue, when possible, to encourage the growth of native foods by selectively harvesting, tilling, burning, pinch pruning, sowing, weeding, and transplanting "wild" plants.

Fresh young prickly pear cactus pads, despined with a carrot peeler.
Photo by Fred Sproul.

Gathering Mushrooms

GAYLEN D. LEE, WESTERN MONO

After the winter rains we begin gathering most of the mushrooms. Mushrooms are one of the few foods my family still gathers annually. Many non-Indians are afraid of mushrooms because some varieties are poisonous, but as Mom says, "We know what to pick and when to pick. Someone else would go up and not know and could get sick."

In the old days, women knew it was time to gather mushrooms when oak leaves began sprouting. Many newcomers to the area bemoan the foggy days that accompany spring, when the clear early morning sunlight suddenly disappears as the fog lifts itself into the mountains. We welcome the fog, whose presence is necessary for some of the mushroom crop to grow...

When it's cold and wet, from November through January, we gather *sekayu*, the fairy ring mushroom. If winter temperatures are mild, sometimes this mushroom doesn't appear until early spring. Regardless, it only appears in a wet year. I think *sekayu* is the best of all the mushrooms. These days we sometimes gather it near Pogoya, which is near Fish Creek Mountain. It's delicious eaten freshly fried or boiled into a broth. Since we pick so many at a time, it's also air-dried and then stored. Whenever we're hungry for *sekayu*, we can cook it into a broth or add it to other recipes.

In the late winter of 1993, after it had rained for days, a bunch of the family drove to Pogoya and had a great day gathering *sekayu*. It had been a long time since the family had been all together, gathering mushrooms. I'm sure each of us was aware of Grandma's and Grandpa's absence. We estimated that altogether we gathered eighty pounds of fresh mushrooms. That sounds like a lot, but after Mom and my wife, Judy, dried the bulk of them, the amount was greatly reduced. There was still plenty to last a long time, though, and to share with others...

When I drive past the many places I went to with Grandma as a child, I still search for rows of white mushroom caps beneath the trees. Or I seek mushrooms in the bulging pine needles on the ground, or watch for a yellow splotch of color on the trunks of oaks.

Ohso (Red Clover)

KATHLEEN ROSE SMITH, YOLETAMAL/BODEGA
MIWOK AND MIHILAKAWNA/DRY CREEK POMO

We picked clover in early spring in meadows.
The nearest clover field was at Lytton Station.
This particular clover field disappeared in the
mid-1950s, shortly after a lumber mill and
holding pond were built next to the field.

Clover is eaten only before it flowers. Pick
the leaves only, no stems. Roll the leaves into
a ball. Add a little salt. Eat it just that way, or
with flank, or wrapped around *béhe*, a baked
peppernut ball (see "Nuts and Seeds"). Sometimes we took the clover home, but it is best to
eat when freshly picked.

Clover, Hopland Rancheria, 1982. Photo by Scott M. Patterson.

Miner's Lettuce and Wild Onions

SYLVIA ROSS, CHUKCHANSI, AND MARGARET VALDEZ, YOWLUMNI

5 cups freshly washed leaves of miner's lettuce, stems
  trimmed
½ cup finely chopped wild onion or green salad onion
2 tablespoons cooking oil

Sauté chopped onion in oil until tender. Add washed and
drained leaves of miner's lettuce and quickly heat through.
Do not overcook. Serve with a garnish of pine nuts.

Wild Onions

LEONA MORALES, MOUNTAIN MAIDU

Wild onions were found along the top of Thompson, Diamond, Eagle Lake, Willard, and Mountain Meadows. We picked them during the spring and summer. The flower is pink and smells like onions. We mix it with acorns but first we cut the tops and boil them, and they are very delicious.

Left: Miner's lettuce, also called Indian lettuce. Right: Wild onion. Photos by Renee Shahrokh.

Yerba Buena Tea

LINDA YAMANE, RUMSIEN OHLONE

A low-growing and exquisitely fragrant member of the mint family, yerba buena has been treasured as a tea and tonic by Ohlone and other Native California people for uncounted generations. ("Yerba buena" means "good herb" in Spanish; its name in Rumsien is *chawrishim* and its scientific name is *Satureja douglasii*.) When gathering, be sure not to over-harvest or pull the plants out by the roots. Just pinch off snippets of the runners, leaving the rooted part of the plant intact. The plant will respond by growing several branchlets and the result will be a fuller, heartier plant. After harvesting, rinse the yerba buena in cool water, wrap in small bundles, and dry before storing. Boil water and steep as you would any other tea. Tea can be brewed from fresh or dried leaves.

Whether I'm hurrying past it in the garden each weekday morning, encountering it on a hillside trail, bending to gather lengths of its nearly heart-shaped leaves, pausing to inhale its intense perfume clinging to my fingers, or sipping a cup of delicious tea, yerba buena always includes memories of my grandmother.

My grandmother, my father's mother, was Beatrice Barcelon (Rumsien Ohlone), born on July 7, 1894, in Tres Pinos. She was the daughter of José Zabalón Barcelona and Alta Gracia Soto (Rumsien Ohlone), the fourth of eleven children. Her mother and grandmothers taught her to gather and use medicinal plants, and throughout her life she used this knowledge to benefit her family and friends. As a boy and young man my father, Robert Gonsalves, helped his mother

and grandmother gather their medicinal plants. Thus, this tradition was carried down through the generations.

I remember Grandma's black zippered "doctor's bag," which she kept well stocked with bundles and bottles of remedies both ancient and modern. It contained Vicks VapoRub, aspirin, and cough syrup, as well as numerous bundles of dried herbs, each carefully wrapped. This was the portable pharmacy of the "Angel of Mercy," as her brothers and sisters called her. She would go to stay with each in turn, when they were ill, to nurse them back to health. Her black bag became well worn over the years.

In her later years, Grandma couldn't gather her own herbs as before. Besides, a modern downtown San José left little living space for native plants like yerba buena. So, when out hiking, I always kept my eyes open for her favorite little mint. It was as good as bringing her treasure. Her face would light up and she'd say, "Oh, Linda!" Then she'd head for the kitchen to put water on to boil and soon her tiny kitchen was infused with a fragrance you have to experience to understand. We would sit and talk, cups in hand, the conversation inevitably leading to memories of her younger years.

Grandma was quite a storyteller, and this was the essence, I believe, of my relationship with her. When I was a child, my grandma lived with us and invented tales full of adventure for the benefit of my brother and me. Throughout the years our bond only deepened. When I was a young adult, we spent a lot of time together, talking or cooking

Left: Beatrice Barcelon (Linda Yamane's grandmother). *Right*: Alta Gracia Soto (Linda Yamane's great-grandmother). Photos courtesy of Linda Yamane.

or tending to any number of chores in her house or yard. And while we worked or ate, Grandma talked. She loved to talk—was actually quite famous for it—and her siblings jokingly referred to her as "a woman of few words."

She told me family stories that spanned her lifetime and beyond, and through her stories I was able to share her life. I came to understand how hard she had worked as a cook for the ranch hands at Rancho Quien Sabe and at the county hospital. I learned that her Papa was gentle and that "Mama" had been quite the disciplinarian. I learned of the hard work and self-sufficiency of her family when they built a ranch in the hills outside Los Baños. And there was the distant grandfather who was killed by a bear.

Her family was full of fun—a downright crazy bunch at times—and we'd laugh 'til we thought we'd never stop at some of the stunts they'd pulled. There was the time her horse threw her and ran off. As she climbed the hill after it, she almost stepped on a rattlesnake, but before the snake could strike she managed to kill it with a rock. When she arrived back at the ranch hours later, the family was frantic because her horse had returned without her, but she carried the rattles as a trophy and as proof of her adventure.

At five-foot even, I've had few occasions to feel tall around other adults, but I towered over my grandma and her sisters. Yet she was a giant in terms of importance and influence in my life. She had a strength that belied her appearance and, like yerba buena, had the ability to survive, even thrive, under varying and sometimes unlikely circumstances. It was through her and her stories that I became firmly rooted to

the area and formed my sense of identity and extended family. It was she who kept the past alive for me.

Grandma died in 1981, and I still miss her. Sometimes in my dreams we are together and I am mystified that she is alive after having been gone for so long. She is more frail than before and it is as though she lives with me. Sometimes I take her to visit her sisters. Other times we are alone and I notice that she is more quiet than when she was alive.

Yerba buena. Photo by Renee Shahrokh.

Top: Roasting agave in a pit.
Bottom: Serving roasted agave.

Roasted Agave Hearts
JUSTIN FARMER, IPAI

Harvest agave plants in their natural growing areas at about 4,000-foot elevation (near the San Jacinto Mountains). Prepare fire in an underground pit and let it burn down to coals. Place agave hearts in the pit. In the old days, the pit was lined with rocks, and they would push hot rocks in on top of the agave, then cover with dirt. Today it's the same except that instead of pushing rocks in, they put sheet metal on, to keep dirt from getting on the agave—people today don't like eating dirt. Roast for about 36 hours. Cool, slice, and serve.

Agave. Photos by Frank Magallanes and Althea Edwards.

Yucca Bread

PAT MURKLAND

Some might think of yucca as a food stuck in ancient times. William "Willie" Pink (Cupeño) of San Jacinto and some young assistants from the San Manuel Reservation near San Bernardino recently demonstrated that this is simply not true. They made yucca bread.

At the annual yucca gathering of San Manuel's Tribal Unity and Cultural Awareness Program in May 2004, Pink showed how:

Start in the spring with a stalk of *Yucca whipplei* (known in English as Our Lord's Candle or Spanish bayonet, and in Serrano as 'umuch). "Get them when they still look like an asparagus, before they flower," Pink advised. "If you get them too late they'll be too tough and stringy."

Bake a section of stalk for four hours in an oven set at 350°. "Once out, you can peel the stem away pretty easily." The section also cuts easily once it has been cooked. Cut it into small strips so you can puree the yucca with a blender. (Otherwise you'll burn up your blender, Pink warned.) Once the puree is ready, you can substitute yucca for pumpkin in a recipe for pumpkin bread. You also can freeze the puree.

Pink and his assistants mixed a crowd-sized batch of bread. The young volunteers cracked one dozen eggs. Precontact Indians had no dairy products, Pink explained, so they would grind up bones to get calcium. Therefore, he concluded with a smile, a little eggshell sent accidentally into the mixture is probably desirable. Pink had already mixed the dry ingredients, including flour, sugar, and spices. Then he blended the wet ingredients into the dry. The mixture was poured into fourteen or so bread pans and carried to the oven by the young volunteers. The delicious loaves of baked yucca bread were shared by all.

Trevor Matthews, James Ramos, Jr., Gabrielle Ramos, and Fawn Ramos, all from the San Manuel Reservation, crack eggs for yucca bread. Photo by Pat Murkland.

Mesquite Punch

KUMEYAAY

4 cups dried mesquite pods
1 tablespoon brown sugar
Pinch cinnamon
Dash of ground cloves

Wash and break up mesquite pods. Cover with water and boil 2 hours, adding water if necessary. Mash frequently. Reserving liquid, wring and break up pods by hand or put through a blender or grinder. Return to liquid and simmer, tightly covered, for ½ hour. To each cup of liquid, add 1 tablespoon brown sugar, a pinch of cinnamon, and a sprinkle of ground cloves. Heat and stir until sugar is dissolved. Serve warm or chilled.

Savory Nopalitos Chips

JANE DUMAS, KUMEYAAY, AND RICHARD BUGBEE, PAYOOMKAWICHUM, WITH FRED SPROUL

If you like Mexican food, you might have tried nopales, or young prickly pear cactus, fried up with eggs and other veggies. Unfortunately nopales don't always win friends, because of their okra-like consistency, which comes from the pectin that is released during cooking.

We decided to make nopales tasty and fun to eat and store—a cactus snack for the modern age—because we often don't wait for a nutritious sit-down meal anymore. So we tried to invent a healthy replacement for potato chips by using a food drier.

As a medicine, prickly pear is recognized to be helpful in controlling diabetes by aiding in cholesterol and blood sugar management; it is known as an immunity builder, and as a poultice for reducing inflammation, pain, and sore gums. Prickly pear has also been suggested as an aid to stimulate lactation. The juice, in particular, high in flavonoids, is used to treat capillary fragility for problems such as colitis, pulmonary problems, prostate inflammation, vaginitis, and diverticulosis.

So how to prepare them? Start with the best! First get some young, flexible pads of the nearly spineless prickly pear cactus called "Indian fig," which was domesticated in Mexico, possibly by the Aztecs. Use a potato peeler to rake off any spines that are there—some people prefer to singe them off over the stove flame.

Then cut the pad into green-bean-sized strips, across the pad from its tip to its base; the longer they are, the better for munching. Lay them out as a single layer on a food-drier tray. It takes about 8 to 10 hours at 135°F before they are crispy and totally stiff and dry. Immediately store them in airtight canning jars. It seems like magic, but 8 to 10 pads can fit into a quart jar. Aunt Jane Dumas loves the natural flavor best, but Fred's favorite is the spicy hot variety he calls "Nopales Intrépido," in which he smothers the fresh strips with hot and spicy marinade before drying. Either way the flavor and benefits of eating cactus will remind you each spring to find some prickly pear in your neighborhood or start some growing in your backyard.

Opposite page, top: Prickly pear cactus chips before (left) and after drying. Bottom: Frozen prickly pear cactus juice (in jars) and popsicles. Photos by Fred Sproul.

BERRIES, FRUITS, and FLOWERS

Sweet and tart berries, fruits, and flowers added flavor and texture to the staple foods of the traditional Native California diet and provided juicy snacks on journeys. Berries were often used to make teas, juices, and ciders. Wild strawberries were eaten raw, while other berries, such as wild grapes and elderberries, were dried and stored for later consumption. In the south, the Luiseño and other tribes peeled the fruit of the prickly pear cactus and let it dry in the sun.

Of course, many people still enjoy these foods. All berries, fruits, and flowers are seasonal, and their first appearance each year marks the change of seasons. In some areas, the first strawberries herald the arrival of spring. Also in spring, Sage LaPena (Wintu) gathers red maids and redbud flowers, which can be eaten raw or added to salads. Renee Shahrokh recounts how, in summer, the bright yellow pollen from cattail flowers can be eaten raw, or dried and used as flour. Lucy Parker (Yosemite/Coast Miwok/Mono Lake Paiute/Kashaya Pomo) dries and stores elderberries—"elder-raisins," she calls them—for use in the winter. And Josephine Peters (Karuk/Shasta/Abenake) enjoys gathering rose hips, which she dries by hanging them over the stove in a paper bag, shaking occasionally so they don't get moldy. The dried rose hips make a delicious, healthful tea that is especially good with honey.

Flowering plants and berry trees supply more than just sweet fruit; they also provide the raw materials for many useful items. The bulbs of several varieties of lily are used for food and soap. Roots, stems, and branches are the essential fibers for baskets. The blue elderberry tree's dried flowers can be used to brew a medicinal tea and crushed to make a poultice; the dried, hollowed stems are fashioned into flutes, bullroarers, and split-stick clappers; and the berries and stems are used to make a black dye for basketry materials.

Yucca blossoms. Photo by Frank Magallanes and Althea Edwards.

Wild Grapes

DAVID W. PERI, BODEGA BAY MIWOK

Prior to the coming of Europeans, when California's Indians were yet sovereign in their own lands, distinctive uses were made of the wild grape. Among my own people, the Miwok of Bodega Bay, ripe grapes were used to bait bird traps and as bait to attract fresh- and salt-water fish. It was said that the sweetness of the crushed grape, when tossed into the water, attracted the fish. Crushed and whole grapes, and sometimes a whole cluster, tied to a string were thrown into the ocean to attract crabs. Having tightly grasped the cluster, and with but a slight tug of the string, the crabs would grasp the cluster even tighter, and they could be pulled in without fear of losing any. Traps for the taking of octopi were made from the vines of the wild grape...

The largest of the green grape leaves were also used by [our people] in cooking meat, fish, shellfish, and fowl, especially when "sealed in" and baked in the underground earth oven. In this type of cooking, the "meat" (meaning flesh of any type) was wrapped in grape or other leaves; or the leaves were used to separate the layers of meat, or as a buffer between the oven's hot inner surface and the meat, to prevent it from scorching or overcooking. In each of these instances, the leaves gave the meat a distinctive taste; even more so when grape leaves were used, and especially when the leaves were used to wrap up the meat—it gave it a delicate acid taste...

Despite the bitter taste, many make the claim that wild grapes make very good jams, jellies, pies, tarts, sauces, and refreshing juice drinks, as well as a rich, full-bodied wine. Many also claim that wild grape jam is more flavorful than its commercial relative, and call attention to the "fact" that a good-tasting jam can also be made using the green, unripened grapes picked in midsummer.

California wild grape, North County San Diego garden. Photo by Deborah Small.

Looking Up and Beyond

Here I stand, head bent down, with my back to the sun, wishing for strawberries. Heat burns my shoulders, sweats my brow, gives me cottonmouth. I imagine heat oozing from asphalt, burning my feet, and smell sweat as I drag myself past glass and steel department stores, then dream of strawberries. I am brushed by the fire buildings and people in buses—we are the inferno of smog and fumes. But enough of time and place. Let us return to the problem at hand. I look at glass, metal and concrete. I taste a world on fire. Strawberries come to mind again. I turn and look past the sun, then shade my eyes, thinking of strawberries and the wetness I will not taste.

—William Oandasan, Yuki

Siblings Blake Parker, Quincy Parker, and Naomi Kashaya Jones (all Yosemite/Coast Miwok/Mono Lake Paiute/Kashaya Pomo) bring berries to be blessed at a strawberry festival hosted by the late Lanny Pinola (Kashaya Pomo) and his family in Point Reyes, 1997. Photo by Beverly R. Ortiz.

Elderberries

RHONDA ROBLES, AJACHMEM

I love to be outside walking in the mountains, along the canyon streams or the hills above the ocean, any time of the year. Fall is the time to look for the deep purple, almost black fruit of the elderberry bush (*kuut* in our language). The health benefits of the elderberry were well known to our ancestors, who always included them in their medicinal pantry. Elderberries (*kuuta*) are said to be helpful for bronchitis, sore throats, coughs, asthma, colds, and constipation. They also induce perspiration to break a fever. Recent research has found that *kuuta* stimulate and build up the resistance of the immune system, and they also directly inhibit the influenza virus. In addition, elderberries are loaded with minerals, antioxidants, and vitamin C.

When I find the right bush I make an offering and a prayer of gratitude for the gifts of the Earth Mother: *Ompaloov Kuut*, or "Thank you, elder bush." Sometimes I like to sing while I gather. I usually cut a small piece of the stem about six inches long rather than picking individual berries; I take a plastic bag to carry the stems, as the berry juice is dark and easily stains. I never take all the berries from one bush, because I want to leave some for others. Once home I immediately rinse the berries on the stem, pat the water off, and hang them together upside down in a warm, dry part of my kitchen. If you cannot hang them, lay them flat on a towel or a cookie sheet. In one to three weeks they shrivel and dry, much like currants. At this point I remove the dried berries from the stems and place them in a small jar. They are now ready to use or store in the freezer.

Our modern lifestyles barely leave enough time for such traditional activities, but this is not a hard thing to do if you like to be outside. Look for the bushes when you walk and find out where they are. They are actually very common all over North America. Learn to identify the leaves, the flowers, and then the berries. Never pick or eat anything that you are not sure about. Avoid picking close to a roadway where cars emit pollution that plants may absorb.

One of my favorite recipes for elderberries is elderberry cornbread, or *kuut* cornbread, made with a package of prepared cornbread mix (I like Trader Joe's, but any will work), one-half to one cup of dried elderberries, and a pinch of dried coastal sage.

Editors' note: Elderberries should not be eaten raw. All parts of the plant contain small amounts of the toxin hydrocyanic acid, which is destroyed by drying or cooking.

Sweet Elder Jelly

RENEE SHAHROKH

6 quarts of blue elderberries
3 lemons
7 cups of sugar
6 oz. liquid pectin

Harvest the berries themselves (purple hands result!) or clip their short stalks off. Don't include any greens! Using a wood pestle, crush the berries through cheesecloth and a strainer, capturing the juice in a bowl.

Sterilize jars and all utensils in boiling water. Drop all lid parts into a separate pot of boiling water and immediately turn water off.

Simmer the juice for about 15 minutes, stirring constantly. Place 3 cups of simmered juice, the juice of 3 lemons, and the sugar in a cooking pan. Bring to a boil, constantly stirring. Rapidly add pectin (6 oz.) and bring back to boil. Boil for 1 minute and remove immediately from heat.

Use a metal ladle to fill jars up to 1/2 inch from the very top. Tighten down lids and invert to sterilize them. Turn them right-side-up in 15 minutes or jelly will be stuck to lids! Cool jars and then check for sealing by pressing on lids. If they pop in and out they must be refrigerated.

Opposite page: Rhonda Robles picking elderberries in Ketchikan, Alaska. Photo by Burt Barlow.
This page: Elderberries. Photo by Laurel Peña.

Rose Hip or Elderberry Syrup
The Haramokngna Potluck Cook Book

3 pounds ripe rose hips (or 3 pounds elderberries)
1 cup honey

Wash rose hips, remove stems, seeds, and ends. Use a stainless steel or enamel saucepan. Simmer 15 minutes or until tender. Mash with a wooden spoon. Simmer another 8 minutes.

Pour into several layers of cheesecloth and allow to drip overnight into a ceramic bowl. Squeeze out leftovers.

Return juice to saucepan, add honey, and blend well. Bring to boil; boil for 1 minute. Pour into jars and seal.

Opposite page: Dried rose hips. This page: Wild rose flower; rose hips. Photos by Renee Shahrokh.

the blackberry grows sweet,
plump and juicy near Williams Creek
it bloomed thousands of years ago
when we savored its flavor first

—*William Oandasan, Yuki*

Huckleberry Bread
Native Cookbook

1 stick butter
1 cup sugar
1 egg
2 cups self-rising flour
1 cup milk
1 teaspoon vanilla extract
2 cups berries (huckleberries or blueberries)

Cream butter and sugar together, add egg, and continue creaming. Add flour, milk, and vanilla. Sprinkle a little flour on berries to prevent their sinking to the bottom. Add berries to mixture. Put in a greased bread pan and bake at 350° for approximately 40 minutes.

Opposite page: Huckleberries gathered by LaVerne Glaze (Karuk), 2001. Pinching off the tips of the branches prunes the bush, stimulating new growth. Photos by Beverly R. Ortiz.

Ernest Siva (Serrano/Cahuilla) harvesting yucca blossoms. Photo by Pat Murkland.

Fried Yucca Petals

The Haramokngna Potluck Cook Book

Flower stalk from *Yucca whipplei*
1 tablespoon shortening
2 medium onions, chopped
2 fresh tomatoes, chopped
1 cup water
Salt and pepper to taste

Pull flower petals from stalk and wash them in lightly salted water. Melt shortening in skillet and add flower petals, onion, and tomatoes. Stir gently until onions are soft. Add water and simmer until most liquid is gone. Add salt and pepper to taste.

Yucca Fruit Snack

KUMEYAAY

Boil fruit of *Yucca baccata* for 20 to 30 minutes. Drain, cool, peel, and seed. Mash pulp and return to pan. Cook until desired consistency for jam. Sweeten if desired. Thickened with flour, it makes a good filling for turnovers. To dry for a snack, spread in thin layers and dry in a slow oven. Roll or fold.

Yucca, Los Angeles County, 2007. Photo by Frank Magallanes and Althea Edwards.

Manzanita Cider

KUMEYAAY

Green manzanita berries
Sugar or honey
Water

Cover green berries with water in a saucepan and simmer 15 minutes or until somewhat soft. Bruise the berries, but do not crush. Let stand overnight. Decant the liquid, let sediment settle, and decant again. Sweeten if desired.

Left: Manzanita berries on the tree. Photo by Laurel Peña. Above: Kathleen Rose Smith (Yoletamal/Bodega Miwok and Mihilakawna/Dry Creek Pomo) gathering manzanita berries, 1989. Photo by Beverly R. Ortiz.

Cahuilla women and children pitting peaches. Photo courtesy of the Braun Research Library, Autry National Center, #LS2034.

NUTS and SEEDS

Nuts and seeds were significant in the traditional diets of many Native California tribes, adding flavor and texture to meals and providing a very dense, easily stored, and highly portable form of nutrients and calories. The single most important food throughout the state was the acorn, which is discussed in the next chapter. Second in prominence to the acorn were the small nuts of pine trees, called pine nuts or piñons (pinyons), depending on which part of the state you're in.

The Serrano of southern California knocked pinecones out of trees with long poles in late summer and early fall, then roasted the cones in earth ovens lined with sagebrush to extract the nuts. The nuts were shelled and eaten whole, or parched, ground into meal, and mixed with water. Besides pine nuts, the Cahuilla also gathered jojoba nuts, or goatnuts, which were roasted, ground, and boiled to produce a drink much like coffee.

Pine nuts are also part of the central California diet. Joan Denys (Esselen) finds new spots to gather pine nuts every year, then brings the nuts to tribal gatherings in Monterey, where they are cracked and eaten raw, or drilled to make beads for jewelry. In the north, hazelnuts were popular. When acorns were scarce—and among the Pomo, even when acorns were abundant—buckeyes were gathered. Like acorns, buckeyes are toxic if consumed unprocessed, so once removed from their hulls, the nuts were ground into flour and their toxins removed in a lengthy leaching process. The Pomo also dried and stored black walnuts, and made arrows, bows, mush stirrers, and other implements from the wood of the black walnut tree. As described in Kathleen Rose Smith's essay, pepperwood (California bay, California laurel) nuts were dried, shelled, roasted, and ground into an oily meal, which could be molded into balls or cakes. Lucy Parker (Yosemite/Coast Miwok/Mono Lake Paiute/Kashaya Pomo) roasts her bay nuts in the oven, cracks off the shell, and adds salt before eating.

In southern California, chia seeds, an important food, were collected with seed beaters in late summer from the small, purple-flowered chia plants. They were transported and stored in burden baskets, then parched and ground into meal. Chia seeds are extremely high in fat and protein, with a slightly nutty taste, and swell to several times their original size when mixed with water. Throughout the state, the small seeds of grasses, red maids, clarkia, sunflowers, and other plants were gathered with basketry beaters or paddles, then winnowed and parched in baskets made specifically for these tasks. Pinole—the meal or flour ground from parched seeds—could be eaten dry or mixed with water, either as a gruel or molded into small cakes.

Chia seedpods, North County San Diego backcountry. Photo by Deborah Small.

Both pages: Leaching buckeyes. Photos by Renee Shahrokh.

You'll Never Go Hungry:
Food Traditions of One Dry Creek Pomo/Bodega Miwok Family

KATHLEEN ROSE SMITH, YOLETAMAL/BODEGA MIWOK AND MIHILAKAWNA/DRY CREEK POMO

The food of my people is important to me. It has sustained us both physically and spiritually since the beginning of time.

I didn't quite realize it when I was growing up in the 1940s and 50s, but my family was a part of that "other America," the poor. As far as food was concerned, however, we always seemed to have enough: fresh fruit and vegetables during the summer; my mamma's home canned food in the winter for fruit pies, jams, and salsa, or as Mamma calls it, "sarsa." Late fall and early winter were the only times the cupboard seemed spare to me; but the lack of fresh food provided some of my most vivid memories of unusual dishes. We had home canned peaches and hotcakes for one memorable Thanksgiving dinner; the syrup was boiled sugar water. Other meals consisted of *pucklon*, which is similar to a dumpling, or fried tripe with mustard greens.

Mamma taught me that we would never starve, because our food, the food that God gave us, is all around; all we need to know is how and when to gather it, how to prepare it.

The teaching included going to the hills and valleys where these foods grow.

I shall always be grateful to my mother, Lucy (Lozinto) Smith, for showing me how to make the foods she learned in her childhood, and from her mother-in-law, Mary (Antone) Santos.

For every year of my childhood, Mamma planted a vegetable garden, no matter where the crops took us to harvest, from the olive groves near Visalia in the south to the fruit orchards of Washington's Wenatchee Valley in the north, and to what must have been a hundred places in between, mainly in central California, southern and northeastern Oregon, and central and southern Washington.

My family also raised hogs, chickens, and cows needed for grandma's blood sausage, stuffed chicken necks with the heads attached, and curds and whey, as well as for the meat, eggs, and milk these animals also provided.

I will always be thankful to my father, Steven Smith, Jr., who died in 1980, for taking me and anyone else who would wake up at four a.m. to the ocean in order to get abalone, which he and my brothers gathered at low tide. I helped by holding the sack the abalone was put into and helping to take it back up the steep cliffs to the car. It was always an adventure, and we'd be home by breakfast.

Mamma, my sisters, and I gathered seaweed off the rocks at other times. Dad would rock fish for bullhead (cabezon) during the day or surf fish at night. Those times, we would camp on the beach and roast potatoes, *tuptups* (similar to pocket bread), flank skirts, and abalone, all cooked on hot coals. The meat was sometimes cooked on a grill we brought along. The coffee was boiled. Cowboy coffee, my dad called it. It was terrible.

We'd drive the long way through Coleman Valley, near Bodega, where Daddy grew up, to catch a breathtaking view of the ocean from iris-clad coastal hills. For this too is a part of the experience of knowing one's place in the order of things.

Daddy loved to hunt, too. But I was never a part of that experience. Only the boys hunted. I fondly remember my younger brother, Doug, shooting robins with his new .22, and Mamma proudly cleaning the birds and roasting them on a spit. *Yah we.* Thank you. Delicious, lovely birds.

I especially want to thank my cousin Olive (Jack) Fulwider for teaching me how to make *béhe*, and for the many other things she has taught and shared with me about her life and her remembrances of our old people.

Peppernuts. Photo by Laurel Peña.

Peppernut Balls (Béhe)

KATHLEEN ROSE SMITH, YOLETAMAL/BODEGA MIWOK AND MIHILAKAWNA/DRY CREEK POMO

Collect ripe peppernuts in the fall when the husk turns purple and the nuts fall from the tree. Next, remove the edible husk (*hat*) so the peppernuts will dry without getting moldy. (My Dry Creek Pomo relatives eat only the tips of *hat* when that part has turned light yellow from green. Later on, all the husk will turn purple, and my Kashaya friends tell me that's the time to eat it. Either way, *hat* tastes like a peppery avocado.) Depending on the weather, peppernuts take several days to several weeks to dry. When peppernuts are dried and ready to be roasted, preheat oven to 350°. Then shell the dried peppernuts; the shells are thin and easy to remove by lightly striking with a rock or small mallet.

The peppernut has two halves. These usually separate when the shell is cracked. If they don't separate, pull them apart by hand. An almost invisible parchment between the kernels will separate naturally from the peppernut if it has been properly dried; if it doesn't separate, it can be removed by winnowing or by rubbing it off by hand.

Place peppernuts on a cookie sheet and roast until they are a rich, dark chocolate brown. When completely roasted, they will look almost burnt. This takes about 20 to 30 minutes. After removing them from the oven, immediately place the hot peppernuts into a blender or grinder. Grind them to a fine, flour-like consistency, then pour them into a bowl.

Season the peppernut flour with sea salt (*tako*) to taste, then knead it while still hot. At first, the nut flour will be powdery and dry. But as the kneading continues, a natural oil in the peppernuts will be released. Once oily, the nuts can be molded into balls about the size of a tablespoon.

As the peppernut balls cool, they begin to harden. When completely hardened, the balls are ready to eat.

Traditionally, *béhe* (peppernut ball, Dry Creek Pomo) is eaten wrapped inside a thick bunch or ball of *ohso* (sweet clover). Fresh endive or green leaf lettuce serve as good substitutes for sweet clover.

Peppernuts

JOSEPHINE PETERS, KARUK/SHASTA/ABENAKE,
AND BEVERLY R. ORTIZ

Josephine usually gathers peppernuts in the middle of October, right after hunting season, when they fall from the trees. The harvest varies from year to year and tree to tree. "They always say every four years is a good nut crop."

After arriving home from the harvest, Josephine squeezes the nuts out of their outer, soft hull, which she considers too bitter to eat. Next, she lays the nuts out to dry. The skin's oily residue helps seal the shell, so the nuts keep longer. "I've had a lot of nuts here for three or four years." Once the nuts are dry, after about two weeks, Josephine transfers them into a cardboard box, bag, or jar, whatever's available for storage.

Roast peppernuts in a 250° oven in a pie tin or cookie sheet for 45 minutes to 1 hour. Open the oven every 5 to 10 minutes or so and shake the cookie sheet, so the nuts roll. "It takes the bitterness out if you cook it slow. We keep shaking them up so they roast evenly." Without shaking, the nuts may burn on one side. Serve whole roasted peppernuts with acorn.

Red Maids

PAUL D. CAMPBELL

The entire plant was pulled up [by Mewuk gatherers] at the end of May and spread out to dry on clean, hard ground or on a granite outcrop. Striking the dried plants sped the separation of seeds. Plants were finally picked up and shaken; seeds were swept together with a soaproot brush, winnowed on a flat, tightly coiled basket. The very rich, oily meal was pressed into balls and cakes for eating.

Red maids flowers. Photo by Renee Shahrokh.

Tossed Wild Salad with Roasted Red Maids Seeds

RENEE SHAHROKH

Indian lettuce greens
Young cattail stalk, sliced
Redbud flowers
Roasted red maids seeds
Oil and vinegar for dressing

Harvest red maids stems and dry them in the sun for a few days. Shake them and the seeds will drop out. Roast the seeds in a frying pan without oil on low heat for a few minutes, stirring them so they don't scorch. Sprinkle the seeds over Indian lettuce and the crunchy cattail slices. Garnish lightly with redbud flowers for flavor. As always, eat wild plants in moderation until you are sure your system is comfortable with them.

Maidu woman using a seed beater. Photo courtesy of The Field Museum, #CSA1835.

Screwbeans and Watermelon Seeds

KENNETH M. STEWART

Screwbean required a lengthier preparation [than other mesquite beans, which were pulverized and made into cakes] before they were edible, since "they don't taste good when they're young, and it takes a lot of work to prepare them." Therefore, it was necessary to "cook" or rot the screwbeans in a deep pit dug in sandy soil for about a month. The beans were covered with arrowweeds, over which water was sprinkled, and they were then covered with earth. When the beans turned red and "tasted sweet," they were removed from the pit and dried on the ground for four or five days. After the beans had been pulverized and ground to flour, a drink was made by adding water to the flour in a pottery cup. Sometimes watermelon seeds were mixed with screwbeans. "They pounded them and mixed them up. Then sifted until it was fine, and squeezed with the hand until it was tight. Just like a real chocolate."

Mojave raft loaded with melons and squash. Photo by Edward S. Curtis, 1907, courtesy of the National Museum of the American Indian.

Pine Nut Soup
Native Cookbook

¾ pound raw pine nuts
4 cups milk
2 cups chicken broth
½ cup green onions, sliced
2 coriander seeds, crushed
1 teaspoon dried mint, crushed
Salt and pepper to taste
Green onions, chopped, for garnish (optional)

Put all ingredients except garnish in a large, heavy saucepan and bring to a boil. Reduce heat to a simmer and cook, covered, for 20 to 30 minutes. Puree soup in a blender or food processor until smooth. Reheat gently and serve with chopped green onions as garnish, if desired.

Note: If reheating after refrigeration, add a small amount of milk or chicken broth to thin slightly.

Sweet Pinyon Muffins
Native Cookbook

1 cup pinyon nuts, ground
½ cup whole wheat flour
2 teaspoons baking powder
½ teaspoon salt
½ cup water
3 tablespoons honey

Combine dry ingredients. Add water and honey and mix well. Pour into greased muffin tins and bake for 30 minutes at 350°. Makes 6 muffins.

Opposite page: Winnowing, pounding, and roasting pine nuts. Photos by Renee Shahrokh.

Sunflowers

THOMAS R. GARTH

Sunflowers of at leave six varieties were used [by the Atsugewi]: *itwisinyami (Balsamorhiza sagittata); tamtiye (B. hookeri); uitsinvami (B. deltoidea);* and *axeiki, giewi,* and *kasnatchup* (these three unidentified). Seeds were gathered in July by beating them into a burden basket with a seed beater. They were parched in a flat tray (*tipwiohi*) and then put into a shallow basket and the skins removed by abrasion against the side of the basket with a rock. After the seeds were winnowed and ground with the mano-metate, they were ready to be eaten. The flour might be molded into cakes the size of a biscuit, which were eaten without cooking. Sunflowers were formerly plentiful on mountain slopes, especially in burned-over areas. A burden basket full of seeds was said to be a good day's harvest for one woman. The gathering might last two weeks.

Editors' note: The sunflowers described here are in the genus Balsamorhiza, *balsam-root. The flowers we usually think of today as sunflowers are* Helianthus, *a different plant.*

Opposite page: Wild sunflowers, Hopland Rancheria, 1982.
Photo by Scott M. Patterson.

Sunflower Bread

Native Cookbook

¼ cup honey
¼ cup butter, softened
2 eggs, beaten
1 cup whole wheat flour
1 tablespoon baking powder
1 teaspoon salt
1½ cups sunflower seeds, ground
1 cup milk
½ cup sunflower meats, whole or coarsely ground

Beat together honey and butter. Mix in eggs. Combine flour, baking powder, salt, and ground sunflower seeds. Add this to the honey mixture and pour in milk. Fold in whole sunflower seeds. Pour into greased loaf pan and bake at 325° for 1 hour. Cool on rack. Bread slices better when cooled.

Chia Gruel

DIANIA CAUDELL, LUISEÑO

Editors' note: Diania Caudell got this recipe from master basketweaver Abe Sanchez. When she and Sanchez prepared chia at the 2003 California Indian Basketweavers Association gathering in Klamath, it was a great success with the elders.

Place ¼ cup of chia in a skillet and roast quickly, until toasted. Do not add any oil or butter. Stir constantly. Do not overcook, because chia will start to pop like popcorn.

Place ¼ cup pine nuts in a different skillet and roast quickly, until toasted. Do not add any oil or butter; stir constantly.

Mix chia and pine nuts together in a food processor and grind into a gruel texture. Place mixture in a bowl and then add honey; orange-sage honey tastes great. You can add fresh ground sage to the mixture for additional flavor. Place the completed gruel into a container with lid and keep in refrigerator.

To serve, I use the stick coffee stirrers. Everyone can get a small amount when needed or to taste. This is instant energy and it tastes great!

At a recent powwow I had a container of chia mixture. Most of the drummers and singers came over for a taste of "candy." It helped them to continue drumming and singing without the aid of coffee or soda. Just natural chia, pine nuts, and honey!

Chia Lemonade

The Haramokngna Potluck Cook Book

> 1 tablespoon chia seeds
> 2 teaspoons lemon juice
> 1 cup natural apple juice
> Ice

Combine chia seeds and apple juice and let soak for 30 minutes until it gets thick, like jelly. Add lemon and ice for a refreshing, slushy drink.

Toasted Chia Candy

BARBARA DRAKE, TONGVA

Use a black skillet or electric fry pan. Put on high heat and add chia seeds. Stir constantly, until there is a great aroma. Take off heat and squeeze in mesquite honey to taste. Break up as it hardens.

Opposite page: Chia flowers, North County San Diego backcountry. Photo by Deborah Small.

ACORNS

Acorns, the nuts of oak trees, have been a California Indian staple for thousands of years. Gathered in autumn, acorns are time-consuming to prepare: a lengthy leaching process is required to remove their tannic acid, but they are highly nutritious and quite bountiful in most parts of the state. Despite the prevalence and convenience of machine-milled, commercially available nuts and flours, many contemporary California Indians gather and process acorns for special occasions. In fact, acorns remain so important that they have become a symbol of California Indian identity.

Tribal peoples gather acorns from at least ten of the twenty species of oak present in California, with black oak, white oak, and tan oak being preferable. In the old times, acorns were stored in elevated granaries and pounded into flour by hand in bedrock mortars. Today, as Ronald W. Lincoln, Sr., (Wailaki/Konkow/Pomo) says, "We're modern, we use whatever is available; we dry them using cardboard or sacks that we can stick out into the air, or if it's raining we put them by the stove."

Since there aren't many books on the topic, learning how to harvest, process, and prepare acorn is often a matter of trial and error. Julie Tumamait-Stenslie (Chumash) grew

interested in acorns and other traditional foods in her early thirties. At first she stored the acorns in plastic bags, but she found she had to discard them because they stayed moist (and became moldy). Now she gathers acorns in plastic bags but transfers them to paper right away.

Once dried, acorns can be cracked and ground. "I had to figure out myself that acorns turn brown after you crack them open; it worried me at first," recalls Tumamait-Stenslie. She also found it effective to grind and leach small amounts of acorn flour in the blender: "I just fill it up with water and pour it off. This way, even if it takes a long time, it makes me feel that I am still doing it the old way."

The most common meal made with acorns is a mush, or porridge, made by cooking acorn flour in a basket with water, adding hot stones to heat the mixture (see "*Wiiwish on the Stove*" in this chapter for a modern version) and generally consumed with meat. Acorn flour was also dried or baked into breads and cakes.

Some California Indians cite their consumption of acorn as the reason for their health or longevity. Patrick Renick (Pomo) is in his sixties but says he doesn't "look or feel it." When asked how he retains his youthful vigor, he credits acorns and seaweed. Perhaps it's the activity of gathering,

Acorn mush at the California Indian Basketweavers Association gathering, 1997. Photo by Robert Dorame and Jan Nichols.

Julia Parker (Coast Miwok/Kashaya Pomo) winnows black oak acorns.
Photo by Beverly R. Ortiz.

or the nutritious all-natural preparations, or the comfort of consuming a food with such great cultural meaning. Renick says that when elders are in the hospital, they often ask for acorn mush, and he likes to bring it to them. "First I used to fight with the doctors and nurses [about it]...Then I asked them, well, if I prove it, will you let me give them the acorns? And I'd have a piece of paper in my pocket from UC Berkeley that broke it down into different compounds nutrition-wise." Even so, he's had to "sneak it into the hospital in a ziplock bag, but it cheered [the elders] up."

Ti-Le-Li: Northern Mewuk Acorn

KIMBERLY R. STEVENOT, NORTHERN SIERRA MEWUK

Acorns are gathered in the fall, at the peak of the season, which depending on weather is toward the beginning of November or sometimes sooner. There are two drops for the acorn, the first of which occurs from September to October. We disregard this first fall. These acorns are normally the wormy ones. Sometimes we will gather these *pehepes* (the Maidu word for clown, or odd, disfigured acorns, due to the worm inside) and use them in our dance regalia. The second drop is the crop we harvest, because these nuts are usually free of insects.

My family and I have been known to gather tons of acorn. I can remember great family outings where we would go and gather together. With ice chests filled with bologna clubs, commodity cheese, white bread, and sodas, we could gather for hours. In the past my Great-auntie Mary had a room in her house where we would deposit all of the acorn we gathered. Our mother did the same in her two-story home. This was a 10' x 12' room, with a four-foot-high board across the doorway. This room was always full of acorn. As children we used to fight for the right to jump into the acorns and stir them up. Lacking a spare room for my acorn, I store mine in gunny sacks and hang the filled bags from the rafters in my garage. No matter how you store your acorn, it is essential that you add a generous amount of California laurel to the nuts. Laurel, or bay leaf, is a natural insect repellent and keeps the bugs away.

We let the acorn dry or season at least for a year; this assures that the nuts are well dried. I can remember that when acorn was needed and the last year's acorns were gone, my auntie would lay the new acorns under her wood stove to dry. After this they could be used.

We then crack and hull the acorns. We spread the acorn meats to allow any additional drying that's needed. On the acorn is a red skin, which is thicker in the crevices of the nut. It is very important that all of this skin is removed. We were taught that if we leave any of the red skin in our acorn, it is a sign of a bad cook. When acorn is cooked with parts of the red skin, it is like trying to swallow the chewy part of popped corn. When the nuts are dried, this red skin has a tendency to really cling to the nuts. If you sprinkle a little water on them when they are dry it lifts the skin, making it easier to remove. We use an open twined winnowing basket in this process of removing the husk skin.

Once the acorn is cleaned thoroughly and dry, we begin the hard work of pounding. Acorn is not ground, it is pounded. We do not have grinding rocks, we have pounding rocks. We also have mortars and pestles. The pestles are raised above the hole in the mortar rock and allowed to slide through your hands into the acorn in the mortar. Some folks use a hopper basket, which catches the acorns as they hop up and allows them to roll back into the mortar. The basket has a conical shape, like a funnel. Of course this is a very time-consuming process, and you develop wonderful arm muscles. But, let's face it folks, this is now. Today for small batches you can use an electric coffee grinder, and a mill and juicer work wonders for medium batches. For large batches like my sister and I make, we use an electric flour mill. The acorn flour should have the consistency of stone-ground wheat flour.

Once you have your flour ground, you can begin the leaching. In this step you are washing out the tannic acid in the flour. Tannic acid is bitter to taste, and if you can digest enough, it is toxic. Traditionally we would go to the nearest stream and find a sandy area. Here we would form a leaching bed and spread out the acorn flour on top of the clean sand. We would then form a channel, bringing the water to the bed and allowing a steady stream to flow over the acorn, or use other watertight baskets filled with clean water that would be manually poured over the acorn. Cedar boughs are used to allow the incoming water to flow evenly over the flour and, some say, to give it the clean hint of cedar taste. You would allow this to continue for at least eight to ten hours, depending on how much flour was being leached. After eight hours you would do a taste test to determine if it

Pages 100-103: Ursula Jones (Kashaya Pomo/Yosemite Miwok-Paiute/Coast Miwok) demonstrates acorn grinding, leaching, and cooking at the California Indian Basketweavers Association gathering on June 23, 2007, in Nice. Photos by Ira Nowinski. This page: Ursula Jones; pounding acorn nuts into flour; sifting the flour from the nutmeats with a soaproot brush.

was ready. Today we have a raised table made of boards and chicken wire, which we cover with a thick bed of fresh pine needles, and then a clean cotton sheet. On top of this we spread the acorn flour and leach it using a water hose placed on top of a spread of fresh cedar boughs. It still takes eight to ten hours. When the leaching process is complete, the flour will no longer have a bitter taste, but rather a slightly sweet nutty taste. When it is ready, we pick it up off the leaching bed. It comes up like globs of wet clay. Using the traditional method of a sand bed, you would gently wash off any sand with water. Because acorn is high in oil, not much sand adheres to it.

The leached acorn flour is then mixed with water, usually a two-to-one ratio for a thick soup or a three-to-one ratio for a thinner soup. This is an approximate measure, as my sister and I mix the flour and water with our hands and know what we are looking for. My sister and I still cook acorn in the traditional method, using baskets and hot rocks. The baskets used for cooking are three-rod coiled cooking baskets. In order to use these baskets for cooking they must be soaked in water overnight. This allows the basket material to absorb water, making the basket watertight. Before cooking acorn we take a little of the leached flour and

This page: Pouring water into the ground flour to leach it; gathering the leached flour; leached flour in the cooking basket.

rub it into the weave of the basket to assure no leakage. We then mix the leached acorn flour with water in the basket.

The morning we are going to cook the leached acorn, we build a large fire in the cooking fire pit. The fire is built upon a stack of cooking rocks. They can be either basalt or soapstone; any other type of rock will burst and crumble. Whatever you choose to use, you always count them before building your fire. Your fire is a clean fire, built of clean wood. Do not use petroleum products to start your fire, and never, never throw trash of any sort into a cooking fire. We use only oak or manzanita wood, as these woods burn hot and leave little ash. We keep this fire burning hot for at least a couple of hours.

When we are ready to cook, the cook's helper will lift the cooking rocks out of the fire one at a time, using large sticks, called *pinita*, made of young cedar or oak saplings. Each rock is dipped into a vessel of water to wash off the ash, then a second vessel to assure its cleanliness. The rock is then placed on the waiting paddle or stirring loop that the cook holds. The cook then gently lowers the rock into the mixed acorn flour. It takes approximately eight to ten rocks the size of an adult's fist to bring a basket full of acorn soup to a full

Both pages: Lowering hot rocks into the basket; stirring the rocks to make sure they don't burn the bottom of the basket; removing the rocks; Jones, with her grandmother, Julia Parker (Coast Miwok/Kashaya Pomo), daughter Naomi Jones, and son Parker Jones (both Yosemite/Coast Miwok/Mono Lake Paiute/Kashaya Pomo), tasting the acorn mush.

rolling boil. The cook keeps the rocks in constant motion. This assures that the basket is not scorched or burned. The cooking process takes about fifteen to twenty minutes. The baskets used are about as large as, if not larger than, a large stock pot. This is a very efficient method of cooking.

When the acorn soup, or *nupa*, is done, the cook removes the hot rocks from the soup. Sometimes the cook will drop the rocks onto clean cedar boughs and allow the acorn adhered to them to bake, making what my kids call acorn chips. Other times the cook dips her hand into clean water and cleans off each rock as she takes it out of the soup, then drops it onto the earth to allow it to cool and bake itself clean.

Acorn is high in protein and contains almost every essential vitamin. We know this because we had to have it analyzed before the doctors at Oak Knoll Naval Hospital would let my grandmother eat it. Hospitalized there before her passing, she wanted to have some acorn. The doctors would not allow her to have it unless it was tested. They were amazed at its nutritional values. We were told that a person could survive on acorn soup and water. As if we weren't aware of this already...

Wiiwish on the Stove
The Haramokngna Potluck Cook Book

Today you can cook *wiiwish* on your stove in a stainless steel or ceramic pan. Don't use iron or aluminum, it will change the color of your *wiiwish*. Bring 4 cups of water to a boil. Put approximately 2 cups of processed acorn flour in a large bowl. (If you don't have time for acorn preparation, you can purchase acorn flour at Korean grocery stores.) Stir it with a spoon to release the oil in the acorn. It is important to add cold water to the acorn flour so that it pours easily into boiling water—acorn flour will clump in the boiling water if it is not mixed with water first. The cold-water-and-acorn mixture should be the consistency of thin gravy. Continue to mix while pouring mixture into boiling water. The acorn flour will start to thicken as soon as it hits the boiling water, so stir constantly—a whisk works best. Turn down heat and bring the mixture to a rolling boil. Cook the acorn for 20 minutes, until you see bubbles on top and it starts to rise, and water has evaporated. It should be the consistency of thick pudding.

Opposite page: Amora Stevenot (Northern Sierra Mewuk), sifting acorn flour at the California Indian Basketweavers Association gathering, 1997. Photo by Robert Dorame.

Acorn Flour for Acorn Mush
Native Cookbook

Hull acorns and spread out to dry for a few days during warm weather. (Acorns may be stored at this dried-whole stage in cardboard containers, such as oatmeal boxes.)

Grind acorns in blender, food mill, or food processor until powdery. If you prefer, leave some chunky bits in.

Leaching procedure: Line a colander with a cloth dish-towel or flour-sack type of material. Put in the acorn flour, and set it in the sink where water will be able to drain through.

Pour water over the flour until it's well covered and leave to drain. Periodically, throughout the day, return to pour water over the flour, perhaps once an hour. This will leach out the tannic acid that occurs naturally in acorns and take out the residual bitter taste of the acid. Note: acorns should not be eaten unless they are leached first.

Acorn flour should be ready to use by evening time. Acorn flour may be stored in covered containers in the refrigerator for later use.

The late Margaret Baty (Auberry Mono) processed acorn kernels into flour using a corn grinder modified with an electric motor by her son and brother-in-law, 1989. Photo by Beverly R. Ortiz.

Above: Acorns being cracked at the California Indian Basketweavers Association gathering in Pala, 2005. Opposite page: Oak trees in the Central Valley. Photos by Dugan Aguilar.

Claiming Acorns
CORA DU BOIS

If a [Wintu] man wandering in the mountains discovered a tree heavily laden with acorns and believed that no one else was likely to find it, he claimed the whole tree and established his right by encircling the trunk with sticks leaned diagonally against it. If the tree was likely to be found by others, he might mark off only a single heavily loaded branch by leaning a single stick against the trunk under the branch claimed. If another man had previously observed the tree but had failed to mark it, he could now remove one stick and place his own there; but he must pay the original marker.

Preparation of Acorn (Wiiwish)

DIANIA CAUDELL, LUISEÑO

Finely ground acorns
Bucket
Colander
Cheesecloth
Clothespins
Medium-sized pot

Measuring cup
Spatula
Wire whisk
Glass of water
9 x 12 inch pan

Step One: Place colander on top of open end of bucket. Drape cheesecloth over colander and press into bowl of colander. Pin cheesecloth to rim of colander using clothespins. Pour finely ground acorn flour into center of colander. Fill medium-sized pot with hot water and pour evenly over the acorn flour. Let drain thoroughly. Repeat this process while gently scraping mixture back to center of colander. When bucket is almost full, but not touching bottom of colander, pick up colander and empty bucket. Place colander back on top of bucket and leach flour one more time. A taste test can be done now. If mixture tastes bitter, leach one more time, then leach again. After final leaching, let mixture drain thoroughly. It will be thick and mushy. Scoop into a medium-sized pot, it's time to cook!

Step Two: Have a glass of water near you for testing. Set burner to medium and remember to stir constantly while cooking. Pour about one and a half cups of lukewarm water into mixture and continue stirring. Mixture will start to thicken and may start to become lumpy. If this happens, add more water. Always keep stirring and scraping sides of pot. Bring mixture to a rolling boil and turn heat to low. Keep stirring over low heat a while longer. Drop a small dab of mixture into a glass of water. If it is ready, it should ball up and float; if not, continue a bit longer and keep stirring. Test again.

Step Three: When the mixture is ready, immediately pour it into a 9 x 12 inch pan. Pour and spread evenly. It will set quickly. Set pan on a cooling rack and cool completely, then wrap in plastic wrap or cover with pan cover and place in refrigerator. Cut into bite-size pieces and serve cold.

Acorn Pine Nut Bread

The Haramokngna Potluck Cook Book

1 cup acorn flour
1½ cups wheat flour
3 teaspoons baking powder
¼ teaspoon baking soda
½ teaspoon salt
1 cup chopped pine nuts or hazelnuts
¼ teaspoon cinnamon
¼ teaspoon nutmeg
2 eggs, beaten
¼ cup salad oil
¾ cup honey
¾ cup milk
1 teaspoon vanilla

Grease a loaf pan (9 x 5 x 3 inch). Sift wheat flour with baking powder, baking soda, spices, and salt. Mix well with acorn flour.

Combine eggs, oil, honey, vanilla, and milk, and blend well.

Add flour mixture to oil mixture; stir in nuts.

Bake at 350° for 1 hour or until toothpick comes out clean. Do not overcook. Let cool for 10 minutes in pan. Remove and cool on rack. Bread will keep in foil for one week in the refrigerator. Freezes well.

Acorn Roca Bars

The Haramokngna Potluck Cook Book

1 cup butter or margarine
1 cup brown sugar
1 egg
1 teaspoon vanilla
2 cups flour
½ teaspoon salt
¾ cup finely chopped, leached acorns
12 oz. milk chocolate or semi-sweet chocolate pieces
½ cup sweetened shredded coconut

Preheat oven to 350°. Cream together butter and brown sugar. Blend in egg and vanilla. Add flour and salt. Stir in ½ cup acorns and spread the thick mixture in an ungreased 10 x 15 inch pan. Bake for 40 minutes. Remove from oven and spread chocolate over the cookie mixture, smoothing as it melts. Mix together remaining acorns and coconut and sprinkle on top of the melted chocolate. Cut and cool.

Wood-Brown Jewels

ELEANOR BEEMER

November 8, 1960. According to my custom of many election days, I picked up Luiseño friends from La Jolla Reservation and took them in my car to their polling place at the Palomar Mountain Post Office, a distance of eight or nine miles to an elevation of five thousand feet. After all had voted, we had leisure for "picking" acorns in woods and along roadsides from among fallen leaves and the still green bracken stalks. Warm sun shone from the blue sky. We had still air and quiet talk. We dragged our burlap sacks along, filling them with only perfect nuts, none of the pinholes of whatever parasite competes for the big nuts with gray squirrels, woodpeckers, and us. If you took a handful and paused to admire them closely, you saw their covering of white fuzz. But if you carried two or three in your hand a few minutes to roll together and stroke and then looked again at them, you found you had brilliantly polished, rich, wood-brown jewels.

Black oak acorns, Palomar Mountain State Park. Photo by Deborah Small.

Buckeyes in October, Mendocino County, 1982. Photo by Scott M. Patterson.

CONTRIBUTORS

Dugan Aguilar (Paiute/Pit River/Maidu) is a professional photographer and frequent contributor to *News from Native California.*

Richard Bugbee (Payoomkawichum) grew up in Old Town San Diego. He is chair of the Advocates for Indigenous California Language Survival, news editor for Kumeyaay.com, and an ethnobotanist under the guidance of Kumeyaay plant specialist Jane Dumas.

Jane Dumas samples prickly pear cactus chips. Photo by Fred Sproul.

Diania Caudell (Luiseño) is a basketweaver and board member of the California Indian Basketweavers Association. Active in education and Indian cultural preservation, she has long fought to preserve the native plants and environments of San Diego County.

Margaret Dubin is the managing editor of *News from Native California,* author of *Native America Collected: The Culture of an Art World* (University of New Mexico Press), and editor of *The Dirt Is Red Here: Art and Poetry from Native California* (Heyday Books).

Jane Dumas (Kumeyaay) is a lineal descendant of Chief Manuel Hatam, leader of the Kumeyaay village once located in the Balboa Park area of San Diego. In 1981 she helped found the San Diego American Indian Health Center, working first as a home health aide and then as a traditional medicine specialist. She and Richard Bugbee teach classes in ethnobotany at Kumeyaay Community College on the Sycuan Indian Reservation.

Richard Bugbee cooks beavertail cactus and onions. Says Richard, "I was impatient and it came out 'cactus al dente,' but it was still good." Photo by Garth Wadsworth.

Justin Farmer at the Karuk Basketweavers gathering in Happy Camp, April 7, 2007. Photo by Allie Hostler.

Justin Farmer (Ipai) is a retired traffic engineer and self-described "incorrigible collector (and maker) of Mission Indian baskets." He is the author and coauthor of books and articles on cradleboards, deer hunting, and Indian basketry.

Debra Utacia Krol (Salinan/Esselen), marketing communications manager at the Heard Museum, is also a member of the Native American Journalist's Association and a book reviewer for *Native Peoples* magazine.

Deb Krol sifts acorn flour at a museum demonstration in Phoenix, Arizona. Photo courtesy of Deb Krol.

Frank Magallanes and **Althea Edwards**, photographers and members of the Ti'at Society, have been documenting activities of southern California tribes for the past eight years. They always look forward to trying new and unusual foods and highly recommend the roasted agave.

Bradley Marshall (Hupa) is the tribal outreach coordinator at the Phoebe Apperson Hearst Museum of Anthropology at the University of California, Berkeley. He is an accomplished artist, regalia maker, and dancer.

Pat Murkland is editor of Ushkana Press, the publishing arm of Dorothy Ramon Learning Center, Inc., a nonprofit, public-benefit corporation dedicated to saving and sharing southern California's Native American cultures.

Bradley Marshall. Photo by Margaret Dubin.

Beverly R. Ortiz is a writer, photographer, ethnographic consultant, university lecturer, and park naturalist who has worked with California Indians for more than twenty-five years. She has published one book and more than 120 articles with and about California Indians, many featuring foods.

The late Scott M. Patterson studied anthropology with David W. Peri at Sonoma State University and went on to work as an ethnographer, ethnobotanist, and photographer until his death in an automobile accident in 1986. His black-and-white photographs of the landscapes and Native peoples of Mendocino, Sonoma, and Lake counties were published posthumously in A Sense of Place: California North Coast Ethnographic Photography (Grace Hudson Museum/Mendocino County Museum: 1989).

Laurel Peña writes about, photographs, and enjoys life on the Klamath River in northern California, where traditional ways and knowledge are helping to restore the world.

The late David W. Peri (Bodega Bay Miwok) was chair of the anthropology department at Sonoma State University and a cofounder of News from Native California.

Josephine Peters (Karuk/Shasta/Abenake), mother and guardian to thirty-one children, is a businesswoman, cultural consultant, educator, artisan, herbalist, gardener, and great cook. Her basketry, basketry-themed pottery, and jewelry are housed in several museum collections.

Hillary Renick dries seaweed in front of her home. Photo courtesy of Hillary Renick.

Hillary Renick (Fort Bragg Pomo/Paviotso Paiute) is a student at the University of Oregon School of Law. She lives with her daughter, Aryana, and when not at school she works to protect sacred sites.

Josephine Peters at the Karuk Basketweavers gathering in Happy Camp, April 8, 2006. Photo by Allie Hostler.

Sylvia Ross. Photo courtesy of Sylvia Ross.

Rhonda Robles (Ajachmem) was raised in Long Beach when it was a rural town. She learned to love the mountains while hiking with her mother. She still returns as often as she can and is sometimes blessed with a full berry bush or the sight of a deer.

Jacquelyn Ross (Jenner Pomo/Coast Miwok) works at the University of California, Davis, and enjoys helping Native people prepare for college and other forms of higher education.

Renee Shahrokh works on pine-nut beads in preparation for teaching a class at the California Academy of Sciences, San Francisco. Photo by Geoff Preston.

Sylvia Ross (Chukchansi) interviewed **Margaret Valdez** (Yowlumni), an elder at the Tule River Indian Reservation, in the summer of 2004, just weeks before Valdez passed away. Descended from Oc-Chee-Lee of the Chukchansi tribe of eastern Madera County, Ross is a frequent contributor to *News from Native California* and is the author/illustrator of *Lion Singer* (Heyday Books).

Renee Shahrokh is an ethnobotany professor at American River College and lectures on the traditional uses of plants by Native tribes in California.

Deborah Small is an artist, writer, and teacher, and one of the cofounders of the Indian Rock Native Garden Project, an ongoing collaboration between art and anthropology students at California State University, San Marcos, and the San Luis Rey Band of Luiseño Indians. She documents the cultural revitalization of Native traditions in southern California, focusing on edible, medicinal, material, and ceremonial plants and their uses.

Kathleen Rose Smith (Yoletamal/Bodega Miwok and Mihilakawna/Dry Creek Pomo) is an artist, writer, cultural consultant, and excellent cook, versed in the plant knowledge of her ancestors.

Fred Sproul is a botanist whose current passion is cactus. He studies Native California foods with Richard Bugbee and Jane Dumas.

Kimberly R. Stevenot (Northern Sierra Mewuk) is a basketweaver and teacher of cultural arts. She lives in Modesto with her husband and three children.

Kathleen Rose Smith gathering redbud shoots, 1991. Photo by Beverly R. Ortiz.

Linda Yamane with freshly picked yerba buena. Photo by Dolores Gonsalves.

Sara-Larus Tolley is a researcher for *News from Native California* and author of *Quest for Tribal Acknowledgment: California's Honey Lake Maidus* (University of Oklahoma Press).

Darryl Babe Wilson (Itami'Is/Aw'te), or **Sul'ma'ejote,** was born on November 21, 1939, at Fall River Mills. He is the author of *The Morning the Sun Went Down* (Heyday Books) and coauthor of *Surviving in Two Worlds: Contemporary Native American Voices* (University of Texas Press).

Linda Yamane (Rumsien Ohlone) is a basketweaver, artist, and historian who has been active in reviving Ohlone basketry, boat making, language, stories, songs, and plant use traditions. She is a coauthor of *In Full View: Three Ways of Seeing California Plants* (Heyday Books).

SOURCES and PERMISSIONS

The following recipes are reprinted with permission from *Native Cookbook* (Berkeley: Center for American Indian Research and Education, 1998): Fresh Smelts, Abalone Chowder, Barbecued Clams, Seaweed Broth, Huckleberry Bread, Pine Nut Soup, Sweet Pinyon Muffins, Sunflower Bread, Acorn Flour for Acorn Mush.

The following recipes are reprinted with permission from *The Haramokngna Potluck Cook Book, Volume 1*, by Barbara Drake and Kat High (Topanga, Calif.: Haramokngna American Indian Cultural Center, 2004): Fried Yucca Petals, Rose Hip or Elderberry Syrup, Chia Lemonade, Toasted Chia Candy, *Wiiwish* on the Stove, Acorn Pine Nut Bread, Acorn Roca Bars.

All William Oandasan poems are reprinted from *Round Valley Songs* (Minneapolis: West End Press, 1984), except "Looking Up and Beyond," which is reprinted from *American Indian Culture and Research Journal*, where the late Oandasan was senior editor.

Essays and excerpts were reprinted from the following sources:

"Medicine for Salmon," from Richard Keeling, *Cry for Luck: Sacred Song and Speech among the Yurok, Hupa, and Karok Indians of Northwestern California* (Berkeley: University of California Press, 1993), pp. 163–164.

"Traditional Pomo Fishing," reprinted from Frank Essene, Eastern (Hopland) Pomo field notes, books XVI-XVIII (manuscript), 1935. Bancroft Library, University of California, Berkeley.

"How Eel Lost Its Bones" reprinted from Susan Calla, Sandra Jerabek and Loren Bommelyn, *Passing the Moon Through 13 Baskets* (Crescent City: Redwood Economic Development Institute, 2005), p. 16.

"Mussels: A Gift from the Ocean," by Jacquelyn Ross, reprinted from *News from Native California*, vol. 10, no. 4 (Summer 1997), pp. 23–24.

"Gathering Shellfish," from Florence Connolly Shipek, *Delfina Cuero: Her Autobiography, An Account of Her Last Years, and Her Ethnobotanic Contributions* (Menlo Park, Calif.: Ballena Press, 1991), pp. 28–29.

"The Origin of Abalone," from Gladys Nomland, *Bear River Ethnography*, University of California Anthropological Records, vol. 2, no. 2 (Berkeley: University of California Press, 1938).

"Abalone: A Precious Gift," by Kathleen Rose Smith, reprinted from *News from Native California*, vol. 4, no. 3 (Spring 1990), pp. 14–15.

"Ingeniously Roasted Barnacles," from Robert E. Greengo, "Shellfish Foods of the California Indians," *Kroeber Anthropological Society Papers* vol. 7 (1952), pp. 63–114.

"Porcupine," told by Viola Williams and Ron Morales in Simmons et al., "Honey Lake Maidu Ethnogeography of Lassen County, California," in the *Journal of California and Great Basin Anthropology*, vol. 19, no. 1 (1997), pp. 27–28.

"Quail and Doves," by Kenneth M. Stewart, "Culinary Practices of the Mohave Indians," reprinted from *El Palacio*, vol. 75, no. 1 (1968). Stewart interviewed Mojave people in Needles, California, and on the Colorado River Reservation, near Parker, Arizona. His main consultants were Peter Lambert, Lute Wilson, Tom Black, and Mrs. Abraham Lincoln.

"Lake Turtles," from Samuel A. Barrett, *Material Aspects of Pomo Culture*, Bulletin of the Public Museum of the City of Milwaukee, vol. 20, pt. 1 (Milwaukee: Public Museum of the City of Milwaukee, 1952), p. 105.

"Bodega Bay Acorn Beef Stew," by David W. Peri, reprinted from *News from Native California*, vol. 1, no. 4 (Sept./Nov. 1987), p. 23.

"Gathering Mushrooms," from Gaylen D. Lee, *Walking Where We Lived: Memoirs of a Mono Indian Family*. (Norman: University of Oklahoma Press, 1998), pp. 93–95.

"Wild Onions," told by Leona Morales in Simmons et al., "Ethnogeography of Lassen County, California," in the *Journal of California and Great Basin Anthropology*, vol. 19, no. 1 (1997), p. 22.

"Yucca Bread" is reprinted with permission from *Heritage Keepers*, the newsletter of Dorothy Ramon Learning Center, Inc., vol. 1, no. 3 (Summer 2004), p. 5.

"Wild Grapes," by David W. Peri, reprinted from *News from Native California*, vol. 2, no. 4 (Fall 1988), pp. 8–9.

"You'll Never Go Hungry: Food Traditions of One Dry Creek Pomo/Bodega Miwok Family, by Kathleen Rose Smith, reprinted from *News from Native California*, vol. 4, no. 2 (Winter 1990), pp. 4–5.

"Red Maids," from Paul D. Campbell, *Survival Skills of Native California* (Salt Lake City: Gibbs Smith, 1999), p. 163.

"Screwbeans and Watermelon Seeds," by Kenneth M. Stewart, "Culinary Practices of the Mohave Indians," reprinted from *El Palacio*, vol. 75, no. 1 (1968), pp. 26–37.

"Sunflowers," from Thomas S. Garth, *Atsugewi Ethnography*, University of California Anthropological Records, vol. 14, no. 2 (Berkeley: University of California Press, 1953), p. 140.

"Claiming Acorns," by Cora Du Bois, *Wintu Ethnography*, University of California Publications in American Archaeology and Ethnology, vol. 36, no. 1 (Berkeley: University of California Press, 1935), pp. 9–21.

"Wood-Brown Jewels," by Eleanor Beemer, *My Luiseno Neighbors* (Ramona, Calif.: Acoma Books, 1980), p. 46.

HEYDAY INSTITUTE

Since its founding in 1974, Heyday Books has occupied a unique niche in the publishing world, specializing in books that foster an understanding of the history, literature, art, environment, social issues, and culture of California and the West. We are a 501(c)(3) nonprofit organization based in Berkeley, California, serving a wide range of people and audiences.

We thank the following for their help in launching and supporting Heyday's California Indian Publishing Program:

Anthony Andreas, Jr.; Barona Band of Mission Indians; Fred & Jean Berensmeier; Joan Berman; Black Oak Casino; Buena Vista Rancheria; Candelaria Fund; Columbia Foundation; Colusa Indian Community Council; Lawrence Crooks; Judith & Brad Croul, in memory of Harry Fonseca; Laura Cunningham; Patricia A. Dixon; Elk Valley Rancheria; Federated Indians of Graton Rancheria; Fleishhacker Foundation; Marion E. Greene; Walter & Elise Haas Fund; Hopland Band of Pomo Indians; LEF Foundation; Robert Levitt; Middletown Rancheria Tribal Council; Morongo Band of Mission Indians; National Endowment for the Arts; River Rock Casino; Deborah Sanchez; San Francisco Foundation; Sandy Cold Shapero; Ernest & June Siva; Orin Starn; Tomioka Family (in memory of Taeko Tomioka); Tom White; Harold and Alma White Memorial Fund.

For more information about Heyday Institute, our publications and programs, please visit our website at www.heydaybooks.com.